From the Backbooth at Chappy's

Other Books by David Housel

Saturdays to Remember

From the Desk of David Housel

The Complete Aubie Story (with Phil Neel)

Tigerettes, Tigresses, Lady Tigers, Tigers
A History of Women's Athletics at Auburn

The Auburn University Football Vault

The Alabama-Auburn Rivalry Vault (with Tommy Ford)

From the Backbooth at Chappy's

Stories of the South: Football, Politics, Religion, and More

War Eagle!

DAVID HOUSEL

David Housel

Copyright © 2021 David Housel.

All rights reserved. No part of this book may be used or reproduced by any means, graphic, electronic, or mechanical, including photocopying, recording, taping or by any information storage retrieval system without the written permission of the author except in the case of brief quotations embodied in critical articles and reviews.

This book is a work of non-fiction. Unless otherwise noted, the author and the publisher make no explicit guarantees as to the accuracy of the information contained in this book and in some cases, names of people and places have been altered to protect their privacy.

Archway Publishing books may be ordered through booksellers or by contacting:

Archway Publishing
1663 Liberty Drive
Bloomington, IN 47403
www.archwaypublishing.com
844-669-3957

Because of the dynamic nature of the Internet, any web addresses or links contained in this book may have changed since publication and may no longer be valid. The views expressed in this work are solely those of the author and do not necessarily reflect the views of the publisher, and the publisher hereby disclaims any responsibility for them.

Any people depicted in stock imagery provided by Alamy Images are models, and such images are being used for illustrative purposes only. Certain stock imagery © Alamy Images.

The author expresses his deep and abiding appreciation to Kirk Sampson, Todd Van Emst, and Kathy Harker of Auburn Athletics, to Jeff Etheridge of Auburn University Photographic Services, for their help, assistance and sharing of photos, and to Kevin Duval for his friendship and ever present availability when computer issues arose.

Scripture taken from the King James Version of the Bible.

ISBN: 978-1-6657-0038-2 (sc)
ISBN: 978-1-6657-0037-5 (hc)
ISBN: 978-1-6657-0039-9 (e)

Library of Congress Control Number: 2020924930

Printed in the United States of America.

Archway Publishing rev. date: 05/05/2021

To Susan and to those young people here at Auburn and beyond who have shared our lives and allowed us to share theirs.

Every saint has a past, and
every sinner has a future.
—Oscar Wilde via John Claypool

The older I get the fewer beliefs I have,
but the more I believe.
—The Professor
Gerald W. Johnson

Contents

A Word of Thanks and Appreciation xv
Foreword xvii
Introduction xxiii

Miss Etta Brown 1
First Love 5
Peacemaker 9
A Glimpse 11
Buddy, Have a Drink 16
God Doesn't Care 17
Through a Glass Darkly 21
Things That Last 26
Food for Thought 30
Remember? 32
Word Pictures—Pictures in Words 37
Do Animals Have Feelings? 44
Ode to the Green Wave … And Why It Still Matters 45
What Fools We Be 50
Worth Thinking about on a Sunday Afternoon 55

Friendship, a Puppy, a Lasting Legacy	56
A Christmas Eve Epiphany	59
Rhett Butler and the Auburn Tigers	61
Even Beating Alabama Has Its Limits	64
Shades of Green—The Masters	68
The Day After	74
Mother's Day	76
It's Okay to Get Mad at God	81
Ain't No More Iron Bowl	83
Muhammad Ali	88
Father's Day	90
Fourth of July	95
My New York	99
Too Much Football	107
Compromise	112
In Sickness and in Health	113
Offensive Woes	119
Forgive and Forget?	120
The Handshake	122
A Matter of Perspective	125
Lord, Gawd, Dave	127
Turning Seventy	132
Voices	137
The Bear Facts	138
Frustrated Jesus	144
Completing the Circle	145

Listening to the Founding Fathers	147
Was I Wrong?	149
My Hero	154
Trump and the Animals	157
A Dark, Dark Day	159
How I Became an Auburn Man	161
From Lewis Grizzard	163
One Way to Happiness	168
A Word on Behalf of Nick Saban, the Great Satan	170
Worth Repeating	176
Heading West	177
I Was Wrong. So Wrong. And I Apologize.	178
Jack Howell	183
All Hail the Green Wave	186
Jack Simms	188
A Debt of Gratitude	191
In the Beginning	193
I Wish He Hadn't Said It	197
Memories of the Fourth of July	201
The Letter G	203
Kudzu and Football	207
How It All Began	209
O.C. Brown	213
Iron Mike	216
The Forgotten Man	220
On Aging	224

The Man	225
Passing the Torch	230
Anything Can Happen Day	234
Held Captive	239
Wisdom	240
It All Began on a Front Porch	242
Truth from a Soap Opera	247
The Past, Prologue to the Future	248
The Color Purple	252
Another One Bites the Dust	253
Defining Moments	256
He Changed My Life	259
Words to Live By	263
Running Naked through the Streets	264
Alabama Politics	265
Start, Finish, Little or Nothing in Between	266
That Thrilling Day of Yesteryear	268
Good Advice	272
Sad State of Affairs	273
A Divided Fourth	274
Lessons Learned in the Hospital	277
All Good Things Must Come to an End	281
A Farewell to Pat Sullivan	285
Decline of the Methodist Church	291
Ellsworth Steele	292
Missing	295

Favorite Christmas	298
Cody Parkey	302
Neil Davis—A Hero for His Time	303
Class Act	306
One Hundred Days	308
From Generation unto Generation	309
A Matter of Utmost Importance	312
Auburn-Georgia—Still the Best	313
Of Hopes, Fears, and All the Years	319
Role Model	320
Auburn-Kentucky—Something Biblical	321
Letter to the Lone Ranger	323
Gramma's Front Porch	327
April 8, 1974	331
The Ultimate Question	334
The Four E's	336
Young Tanner Bailey	340
I Hear the Train a Coming	344
Would You Do It Over Again?	348
All I Know, All I've Ever Learned	351
Epilogue	359

A Word of Thanks and Appreciation

Special thanks go to Dick Parker, Jason Peevy, and Ellyn Hix for their help in formatting and putting this book together. And to Rheta Grimsley Johnson for her kind and gracious, as always, foreword.

To Brady Adams, Peter Le, and Tim Fitch at Archway Publishing for guiding me through the publication process.

To Charley Van Eaton and Ed Ruzic for their encouragement and insistence that this book be done.

To Backbooth founders Kenny Howard, Francis Sanda, and Chris Brymer.

To the Backbooth regulars, Matt Hersel, Jim Jenkins, Walt Woltosz, Dave Autry, Steve Benson, Jim Dembowski, Jim Dozier, Drew Goodner, Dan Homan, Harry Hooper, Rick Long, Roy Parker, Ken Ringer, Dave Rosenblatt, Russ Suther, John Staton, Chuck Williams.

To the Friday group, Tom Penton, Gerald Johnson, Cory Smith, and Chip Townsend.

To the latecomers, the post-Backbooth group, Jim Mathews, Gary Perkins, Charlie Morris, Eric Ellis, Ernie Hughes, and Dick Dreher. Some of these ideas and thoughts are yours.

To David Barranco, owner of Chappy's, his son, Jeff Barranco, Kevin Rolf, and Michael Callaham, thank you for providing the environment.

And to Cassidy, Courtney, Monica, Mary Beth, Cara, Rosie, Chris, and others who have served us over the years. This book is as much yours as it is ours.

Foreword

David Housel and I don't always see eye to eye.

That never stopped us from having heart-to-hearts.

When he was adviser for the *Plainsman* and I was its editor, there's never been such an odd couple bopping about Auburn, campus and town. Jack Lemmon and Walter Matthau pale. And yet somehow we forged a friendship that has lasted forty years.

He considers me liberal. I consider him conservative.

He would fall in the love-it-or-leave-it camp. Much of the time, especially right now, I'd love to leave it. David loves New York; I prefer Paris.

But despite our differences, we're always glad to see each other. I like to think the friendship is solid because of mutual respect.

Looking back—way, way back to the early 1970s—we were both so young, personalities still jiggling in the mold, and yet, I have to say, we were even then both determined to become who we would become.

He loved John Wayne. I loved Clark Gable.

So we went to see Clint Eastwood. Sat side by side in Midway Plaza Theater and shared popcorn and secrets. He took me to see my first Major League Baseball game in Kansas City and sang "Take Me Out to the Ballgame" all the way there. We ate steaks the size of New Hampshire and drank too much Cowboy Punch at the Golden Ox steakhouse.

David was one of fewer than ten people invited to the wedding when, my senior year at Auburn, I married Jimmy Johnson at Callaway Gardens. David brought us a bottle of champagne. My mother, a teetotaler, had this to say: "And I thought David Housel was a *nice* man."

David Housel, the only real adult in the *Plainsman* office, never once said I could not print a story, or a photo—remember streaking?—or get a little crazy even with the April Fool's edition. I'm sure he didn't agree with everything we ran in the *Plainsman* the year I was editor, nor did his buddies from the Athletic Department who would stop by to complain to him. But David did not consider censorship part of his job. He had been editor too and could see it from both sides.

Back then, we both got a little blue at Christmas and for a long time took turns phoning each other on Christmas Eve. The phone calls ended somewhere along the way, but I always think of David at Christmas. Don't do much about it, but I think of him.

But this isn't really about all of that. It's about this book, his writing, which so many follow and love. He might surprise readers a bit with this collection, especially those of us who haven't been close to David in a long while. His thinking on some matters has evolved, which is how wisdom is won.

David still writes in superlatives, the way most of us dream. The best Saturday. The most exciting football game. The most alluring Mouseketeer and prettiest girl, Annette Funicello. The wisest friend. The kindest woman. The best lead on a sports story.

He writes the way a young boy sees the world, in black and white, with a sense of great wonderment and adventure, a guileless belief in truth, justice, and childhood heroes. Passionately, without too many weakening qualifiers or foreign phrases or other things *The Elements of Style* told us reporters to be sure and avoid.

He calls himself "old" more than once in this manuscript, but he doesn't write "old." He has the eyes of a child, as his Bible might say, and is not burdened with that veil of pseudo-sophistication or overwrought language so many trying to write a book resort to.

He is direct. He is spare. His writing is that of a veteran sportswriter, which he is. A sportswriter who always cared more about the players than the play.

A small town is a big place in David's writing. His hometown of Gordo takes on mystical qualities, and you feel its power. You stand with David and his brother and mother staring through a neighbor's window at their black-and-white

TV. You can see Miss Etta's house where her son Irving was confined by fence wire lest he wander. You meet with appreciation Hat-T, the woman who helped rear David and fed him magnificent hot meals at dinnertime.

His heroes are here in vivid portraits, and not all of them are football coaches. He reminds us of Neil Davis, Evelyn Jordan, Ellsworth Steele, Bobby and Sally Barrett, Fran Davidson, and many other examples of strong character from the Auburn world, including my late buddy Jack Simms.

"He had a heart, a kindness, and a compassion, that he did his best to hide," David writes about Simms, perhaps the best description of the journalist and journalism professor I've seen.

David also reveals fascinating tidbits about the speed of black bears, the storm drain that runs under Jordan-Hare Stadium, the fact that Lt. William Calley used to lunch at the Auburn Grille. And, yes, lest you worry, there are lots of his signature stories about football.

What surprised me? David Housel loves Broadway plays and Time Square. He declares that Muhammed Ali "was a great American." He does not believe God hears prayers concerning football, even before the Auburn-Alabama game. Thanks to C.M. Newton, he no longer hates Alabama. He despises it when Alabama political candidates for any office run on Jesus and against Obama with no other stated platform. When it comes to politics, he doesn't consider himself red or blue but purple, free to vote for "the best candidate" regardless of party.

Don't get me wrong. I still don't agree with David Housel on everything. This old Yellow Dog Democrat read quickly, for instance, his laudatory remarks about Nick Saban.

One night in 1992, I was having a brew in Barcelona at the beer garden built especially for sportswriters covering the Olympics. Not being a sportswriter, I felt a little out of place but was invited to sit with a group of about six men drinking and shooting the breeze. I remember they were from all over, not Alabama but Ohio and Georgia and, if memory serves, Texas and Tennessee. None of them knew me or my Auburn connection.

Before long, the name "David Housel" was mentioned, and all of the strangers started beaming and singing my friend's praises. "Best SID ever," one said, and got a rousing amen. The Housel stories began and continued a long while in the cool summer evening of faraway Barcelona.

David Housel is not just an Auburn legend. He belongs to the world.

Our differences for decades have made our friendship interesting, and I love the man like a slightly older brother. As his mother used to say, "Lawd, God, Dave." This is your best work.

Introduction

As Forrest Gump so famously said of his mother's box of chocolates, "You never know what you're gonna get …" so it is at the Backbooth at Chappy's.

And so it is with this book.

One never knows what the topic of discussion will be when taking a seat with the gentlemen at the Backbooth of Chappy's Deli here in Auburn. The topics change daily, often several times within the same sitting. The topics are broad and know no bounds.

Most of these stories, thoughts, and observations had their genesis at the Backbooth at Chappy's. They remain true to the discussion and sometime ponderings of that day.

As with that box of chocolates, you never know what's coming on the next page. That's the way it is in the Backbooth. That's the way it is in this book. You never know what's coming next.

These are stories of Alabama and the South. There is football, Auburn and Alabama football, politics, religion, all the things you aren't supposed to talk about, and more, a gauntlet of life in Alabama and the South. These are stories about humanity, about people like us, doing the best they can to honor their past and make their future dreams come true. Some do; some don't.

We are all imperfect people living in an imperfect world doing the best we can. These are our stories, these are our times.

Welcome to the Backbooth at Chappy's

Have a seat.

Miss Etta Brown

She came to me last week, and I can't get her out of my mind. Or my heart. And I'm not sure I want to.

She came to me while reading a book selected by my honors college book club. The title doesn't matter—it would only detract from our point.

I first remember her living way out in the country, on the Speed's Mill side of Gordo, on the back, back roads, all dirt, rutty, and usually dusty or impassible—depending on how long it had been since the last big rain. Down in Bostic Beat, as they called it, way down in Bostic Beat.

Daddy used to take us squirrel hunting in the little hollow behind her house. It was a good place to spend the afternoon with your daddy in the fall.

As a matter of courtesy and respect, we would always stop by Miss Etta's house to let her know we were going hunting in the hollow and to ask if that was okay. She never said no.

Miss Etta lived in what today would be called substandard housing, a wooden shotgun house with big porches on the front and back, a dog trot down the middle, and two rooms on either side of the dog trot. It wasn't much—there were worse—but it was her home.

It was there that I first met Irving, her mentally challenged adult son. His mental issues were called a lot of things back then, names and descriptions that would not be used in polite society today. And I will not use them here.

I am not knowledgeable enough or smart enough to understand all of the medical terms used today. But this isn't about medical terms or medical treatment. It's about love, a mother's love for her son. That he was mentally handicapped made no difference. No difference at all.

She could have sent him to Bryce Hospital, the state home for the mentally ill, a mere twenty miles away in Tuscaloosa, but she wouldn't hear of it.

Irving was her son, her God-given son, and she loved him dearly as he loved her dearly, and he depended on her. She was going to be with him and take care of him, no matter what the days might hold, and there were certainly challenges.

It may sound cruel today, perhaps even a little inhumane, but in those days it was an act of love. To keep him from wandering away from the house and into the deep woods, Miss Etta fenced in the back porch and the side of the house to the right of the dog trot. That was Irving's home, a home within a home.

More often than not, to be polite, Daddy and I would go speak to Irving on our way to hunt. He was usually pacing the back porch, making loud, unintelligible sounds and utterances.

We would speak, but Irving never responded. I remember Miss Etta saying once, "Son, he just don't understand." She said it with a smile, not a happy smile but a sad, caring smile, a loving smile. I understood.

As the years went by, Irving aged, and Miss Etta grew old as we all do.

Finally, perhaps after her husband died, I don't know, Miss Etta moved to town. Irving was older now, more dependent on her and less prone to roam. Wire was no longer needed.

They shared each day, the two of them, in that little house just up the hill from the sawmill, warmed by a gas heater in the winter, cooled by an oscillating fan in the summer. On nice days, they would sit on the front porch and, as they say in small towns, watch the world go by. Irving spoke, in reality yelled, to everyone who walked by. Miss Etta smiled and waved, her attention always fixed on Irving.

They would walk to town, such as it was, on occasion to buy necessities, food and household supplies. Irving was always at Miss Etta's side, trying to join in the conversation, but all he could do was utter loud, unintelligible sounds, sounds that may have had meaning for him but a meaning we could not comprehend or understand. It never bothered Miss Etta, but she would, from time to time, gently touch his arm, and he knew it was time to be quiet. He always responded.

In the aforementioned book, noted neurologist Oliver

Sacks wrote case studies of his mental patients, "so broken on the outside, so whole on the inside."

Was that the case with Irving? We'll never know. He was born too soon to take advantage of today's medical advances. But this much is certain—he was loved.

I've never known a mother, even my own, who demonstrated a mother's love more so than Miss Etta.

The Good Book says, "Greater love hath no man than this, that he lay down his life for another" (John 15:13 KJV). Miss Etta Brown lay down her life for Irving.

Irving died, and within a few weeks, perhaps a month, Miss Etta died too. Her race having been run, her purpose for living no more. In whatever the great beyond may hold, she was with her son. She could ask for nothing more.

Fifty years later, few people in that small town remember her anymore. But for those of us who do, one word comes to mind—love.

Love.

Not a bad way to be remembered.

Not a bad way at all.

First Love

It was kind of absurd.//
Really more funny than absurd.

There we were, four old men, ranging in age from seventy-two to seventy-seven, sitting in the Backbooth at Chappy's talking about Annette Funicello.

After all these years, she still had a hold on us.

Annette, of course, was one of the original Mouseketeers on the *Mickey Mouse Club* that aired on ABC every Monday through Friday at four o'clock from 1955 to 1959. Annette was the prettiest, most alluring of them all.

It was the best time of the week because we got to see Annette. And when we saw Annette, our hearts, our minds, our souls, everything about us stirred in ways we could not yet understand.

Thursday was the best day of the week because we got to see more of Annette on our little black-and-white TVs than on any other day of the week. We knew. We had checked it out. Carefully.

And sixty-five years later, here we were, four old men talking about how we loved Annette Funicello.

In later years, we might have called it lust, but at that age, nine or ten years old, we didn't know what lust was. All of that was still to come.

We all thought we were the only ones to love Annette that much. But in later years, we found out that she was the most popular Mouseketeer of all, getting up to six thousand fan letters a month, sometimes a thousand in a week, or sometimes in a day. They came overwhelmingly from preteens like us who worshipped and adored Annette and the ground upon which she walked.

I wrote my share of those letters, sometimes two or three a week, and I must admit to hoping those letters have long since been destroyed.

To my grown-up embarrassment, I remember writing her once telling her how much I would like to meet her.

I couldn't afford to go to California, I wrote, but if she was ever in Birmingham, let me know, and I would see if my parents would drive me to meet her.

Atlanta might be a possibility. That would be harder to pull off, but I would try. Anything to meet you, Annette.

The lengths to which a ten-year-old boy would go to meet a twelve-year-old girl …

That letter must have gotten someone's attention. Not long after that, I received a postcard-size picture of Annette with her signature printed on it.

It was nothing more than a mass-produced publicity shot, but I didn't know that. I didn't know what a publicity shot was.

When that card arrived, it was one of the happiest days of my young life. She knew who I was, she knew I existed, and she knew that I cared. The goddess Annette.

In my youthful naiveté, I thought it was just for me. I was the only one.

Suddenly Birmingham and Atlanta didn't seem so far away.

Now I don't know what I would have done if I had ever met Annette. And neither did any of the other guys sitting in the Backbooth that day.

We would probably have blubbered all over ourselves, but we loved her, and we knew she would love us too, if we could only meet.

We didn't like those beach blanket movies Annette made with Frankie Avalon. She was spending too much time with him, time she could have been spending with us, and at the beach too. To tell the truth, I still don't care much for Frankie Avalon.

And you can put Bobby Burgess, that long, tall, dancing Mouseketeer, in that group too. Childhood jealousies die hard. Fantasies too.

Annette left us in 2013 at the age of seventy, a victim of multiple sclerosis. I never met her, but what a legacy she left.

Four seventy-year-old men sitting in the Backbooth at Chappy's talking about Annette.

That girl sure had staying power.

Peacemaker

C.M. Newton
1930–2018

C.M. Newton was the man who made me stop hating Alabama.

Competitive though he was, and he was really competitive, especially against Auburn, he was always so nice, so sincere, and so kind. So caring. So genuine. So respectful.

There was never anything false or fake about C.M. He was a great coach and an even better man, mentor, and friend. He would always come by—seek me out really—to ask how I was doing and how Susan was doing. Just a good, fine, and decent man.

How could I dislike this man, I finally realized, just because of where he worked? I couldn't.

C.M. Newton caused me to put away childish things and begin to think and act like a man.

As Coach Bryant said of Coach Jordan when he retired in 1975, "It's possible to compete against a man for a day and respect him for a lifetime."

That's how I felt about C.M.

That's how I, as an Auburn man, have come to think about Alabama. Compete with them, yes. Compete with them every day in every way, twenty-four seven, 365, sometimes 366 days a year, but don't hate them. Don't look at them with spite in your mind and in your heart.

It doesn't hurt or affect them at all, not in any way. But it does affect your ability to compete against them in meaningful and effective ways. Learn to give credit where credit is due and go from there.

C.M Newton, by his example, taught me that, to put away childish thoughts, childish attitudes, and I shall be forever grateful.

And tonight, on the day of his passing, I'm glad I told him about the difference he made in my life.

So very glad.

A Glimpse

It was a glimpse. Just a glimpse. But a glimpse of how the world could be and should be.

It was at the Birmingham airport where we were gathered to welcome two new members to the family. Yes, the airport is a strange and unusual place to meet two new family members, but these were not to be ordinary family members.

They were two little girls from the Congo being adopted by our niece and nephew, two of the kindest, most loving and caring young people you could ever meet. The kind who give great comfort and confidence about the future of our country, the faith, and the things that matter.

They had already been blessed with two sweet, young, rambunctious boys, but the Lord put upon their hearts that they could and should do more. The needs of abandoned and orphaned children in the Congo came to their minds again and again. They could not escape it, and it became their calling.

Their sons, seven and eight, were very much a part of the prayer and discussion. It was to be a family adoption, not a parental adoption.

They made contact with a Christian adoption agency, and the long, slow, sometimes grueling process began. There were many delays in paperwork and procedure in the Congo. Two cultures sometimes clash in administrative procedures.

Once the process was underway, they were asked if they would consider adopting sisters, ages one and two, so the two girls could stay together. They prayed about it, waited to be led, and said yes when one of their young sons said, "Mama, if we adopt both of them, they could hold hands."

Having never been to the Congo, they made their initial selection through pictures, descriptions, and comments from the orphanage where the girls were living and the adoption agency that they trusted completely.

Long before they had ever laid eyes on them except through pictures, they loved these two little girls as if they were their own. They soon would be, but it would take some time.

Gifts were given and money was sent to support the girls and to meet their needs in the orphanage. They lacked for nothing. Except for the most important thing: a family to love and a family to love them.

The young couple went to the Congo in the spring, thinking they would come home with their girls. It was not to be. After two weeks of bonding with those they now considered "our girls," they had to come home alone. All of the paperwork had not been signed. Bureaucracy here, bureaucracy there, bureaucracy everywhere, it's all the same.

They came home hurt and disappointed, but they had met and spent quality time with their daughters. Through the miracle of Skype, the girls had met their big brothers, happiness, smiles, and anticipation all around. One day they would all be together as family.

Finally the big day came. The girls came home, and we were all there at the airport to greet them.

Papers and dissertations galore have been written on the pros and cons of international and interracial adoption. And there were concerns and considerations in this adoption too, as there are in all adoptions. But what God has joined together, let not man put asunder.

All the days will not be sunny and bright, some days will be challenging and difficult, as they are for us all. But whatever their days may hold, they will be days filled with love, care, and nourishment.

"My girls are coming home today," the mother said in a Facebook post.

"Now the hard part begins," one reader responded, "the raisin' and the rearin'."

"But," the poster added, "that's part of the blessing. You, your husband and your boys are blessed to be a blessing."

Finally, around 4:19 one Wednesday not long ago, two little African girls came down the escalator to the open arms of their new parents, who gave them long, loving embraces, and to the happy chatter of their two brothers, each eager to be the first to hug them both.

One of the brothers, knowing his new sisters did not speak English, wanted them to hear words they would understand. He learned a phrase in French, the language spoken in the Congo. As they arrived, he said it over and over, again and again: "Bonjour! Bonjour!" which means "welcome."

When I met my new grandnieces for the first time, I didn't see Americans or Africans, black or white, none of the man-made lines that are used to divide. They were just two beautiful little girls with bright, shining, happy, and inquisitive eyes—smiling faces with smiling eyes. It was beautiful, and it was moving.

In that moment, be it ever so brief, there was a glimpse of the world as it could be and as it should be, the universal brotherhood of man, the love of parents for new children and for all of their children.

"I don't know which is worse," the new granddaddy said, "the delivery waiting room or waiting at the airport escalator. It's all pretty special." He teared up as he spoke.

Everyone met and greeted, the once family of four, now a family of six, got into their SUV and headed home. Along the way, they stopped, and the girls were treated to their first American meal, Chick-fil-A.

A new day had begun.

Back row: Kelly and Jim Powell.
Front row: Anna Grace, Mary Grace, Logan and Parker Powell.

Buddy, Have a Drink

The day of Pentecost is one of my favorite days on the Christian calendar. It gives me permission to have a drink.

It's that part about how the people responded when the Holy Spirit, the Spirit of God, came upon them. They were acting differently, all crazy-like, saying things not everybody could understand.

"They're drunk," said one of the disciples.

"They aren't drunk," Peter responded. "It's not even nine o'clock."

"Not even nine o'clock."

What about after nine o'clock? Peter did not seem to judge the act, just the hour.

Taking the Bible literally, as many people do, it would seem to me that it was okay for me to have a drink ... just as long as I was sober by nine o'clock the next morning.

I usually was.

Usually.

That's what the Bible said to do.

God Doesn't Care

God doesn't care about the outcome of the Auburn-Alabama game.

Not one iota.

If He did, coaches wouldn't matter, blocking and tackling wouldn't matter, practice and preparation wouldn't matter, talent on the field wouldn't matter, home field advantage wouldn't matter.

The only thing that would matter from a team concept would be the praying skills of the two team chaplains, Father Gerald Holloway of Alabama and Brother Chette Williams of Auburn.

We make God, the Almighty, the Holy One, into a Santa Claus-god when we pray, "O Lord, please help Auburn win today" or "Father God, help Alabama win." In other words, "Give me what I want!"

Or worse, when we try to bargain with God: "Lord, if you will help Auburn win, I'll never (do this or that) again" or "Father God, if you help Alabama win today, I promise I will always (do this or that) …" Always.

Go ahead and admit it. We've all done it. Some of us still do it.

Even preachers do it. At least one did. At least one admitted it.

I had a Methodist minister friend who believed until the day he died that God helped Auburn win the 1997 game. Alabama led 17–15 and was running out the clock when Auburn recovered a fumble, kicked a field goal, and won 18–17.

My friend, a minister of God no less, was praying that God would not let Alabama upset Auburn. He dropped to his knees in desperation, and at that moment, that very moment, the God who placed the stars in the skies reached down from heaven and stripped the ball from the Alabama player, enabling Auburn to win the game.

I don't believe it.

Praying to win football games is not limited to Christians. A Muslim friend drove all the way across Saudi Arabia, 750 miles or more, to the holy city of Mecca to pray for an Auburn victory over Alabama in 2002.

That was the year Auburn's top running backs, Carnell Williams and Ronnie Brown, were hurt and hardly anyone gave Auburn a chance to win in Tuscaloosa. My friend prayed all day at the Holy Mosque, Islam's most holy shrine, asking Allah to give Auburn the victory. He then drove fifteen hours home, "opened" the television, and saw that his prayers had been answered. Auburn won 17–7.

Alabama fans no doubt have similar stories, perhaps 1967, the rain game and Kenny Stabler's run, or 1985, the Van Tiffin kick game.

My question is this: how does God determine who He's for? Is He for one team, as He appeared to be in 1997 when Alabama fans were thanking Him for answering their prayers and delivering the much-longed-for victory over Auburn?

Did God, the Holy One, suddenly change his mind, cause the fumble, and decide to answer the prayers of my minister friend and Auburn fans? Or was the Almighty toying with Tide fans the whole time, knowing that in the end He would cause them to lose. If He did that, it was cruel, very un-God like.

But, you might be asking, what about that promise we've heard again and again in sermon after sermon all of our lives, that part about asking for whatever we want in His name, and it will be given unto you. That part.

Think about it.

"Jesus, in your holy name, we ask that Auburn beat Alabama" or "Jesus, in your sweet and blessed name, we ask that Alabama beat Auburn today. We beseech you."

Get real.

The outcome of a football game is not something that should be lifted to heaven in Jesus's name.

To do that is more than a sin. It's sacrilege.

We need to remember that verse that says render unto

Caesar the things that are Caesar's and unto God the things that are God's. The outcome of a football game is secular. It belongs strictly to Caesar, not to God. The real God, the one true God, has more important things on His mind, like peace in the Middle East or grieving while His children senselessly kill one another or die of the coronavirus.

Maybe even the presidential election. Some would say so.

There's one final verse to consider, the one that says when a man (or woman) grows up, it's time to put away childish things.

Praying for the outcome of a football game is a childish thing. A very childish thing.

It trivializes the Almighty.

Grow up!

The Auburn-Alabama game is big enough as it is.

We don't need to get God involved.

Through a Glass Darkly

This story has its beginnings a long time ago in a country far, far away, a country I've never been to and a country I never want to go to. In a village. A village called My Lai.

Fast-forward to the early seventies, to The Grille, College Street, downtown Auburn. It was the lunch place of choice in those days, and a man named Calley, Lt. William Calley, frequently ate at our table, a guest of his state trooper friend, Clyde Wilson.

We knew Calley was in nearby Columbus, Georgia, awaiting court-martial for something that happened in Vietnam. We didn't know the details. William Calley was just a guy who ate lunch with us on occasion.

He was a nice guy, a quiet guy, never said much. It is safe to say that most of us around the table thought rather highly of him. Some may have even offered money to help in his defense. I don't know, but it would not surprise me if it were so.

We, most of us, were passionate believers in the war. This man was an American war hero, and we couldn't understand why the army was persecuting him.

We thought he was a pretty good guy.

But looks, as we learned, can deceive.

Years later, we learned the truth, and we learned about the real hero of My Lai, not William Calley but a man named Hugh Thompson from Stone Mountain, Georgia.

When I learned the truth, I felt dirty, ashamed, unclean. How could I have been so foolish? How could I have been duped so easily?

Perhaps for the first time, I had to seriously consider whether what I had always been taught was true. Are the cowboys, the guys in the white hats, always good guys? Do American soldiers, do Americans, always do the right thing?

Here is that real story.

Thompson, an American helicopter pilot, saw Vietnamese civilians being herded to irrigation ditches and then killed by Calley and his men using knives, bayonets, grenades, and small arms fire. For the women, it was worse.

Depending on whose estimate you believe, American or Vietnamese, between 350 and 500 villagers, mostly women, children, infants, and the elderly, died that day, March 16, 1968.

Many more would have died had it not been for the heroic efforts of Hugh Thompson.

Recognizing the horror of what was happening, Thompson knew what he had to do when he saw other villagers cowering in fear as they watched the American soldiers who had killed their friends and family approach.

Thompson landed his helicopter between the Americans and the Vietnamese, told his crew chief and gunner to cover him, got out, and walked over to the American side.

Thompson told the American troops that if they opened fire on the Vietnamese civilians, he and his crew would open fire on them.

Calley's troops eventually stood down, and the killing stopped. Thompson and his crew, with the help of two more helicopters, evacuated the remaining villagers to safety. The My Lai massacre was coming to an end.

There is a museum at My Lai today honoring Thompson's bravery and listing the names of the Vietnamese who died there that day.

Though the military tried to hide the massacre and thereby Thompson's heroics, the story eventually came out, much to America's horror. It is said to be one of the turning points of public support for the Vietnam War.

Thirty years later, in 1998, after being condemned and ostracized by many individuals in the military, government, and public for testifying at Calley's court-martial, Thompson and his crew received the Soldier's Medal, the army's highest award for bravery not involving direct contact with the enemy.

Calley's trial began not long after those lunches at the Grille. He was convicted of killing twenty-two Vietnamese civilians and sentenced to life imprisonment at Fort Leavenworth.

There were, and perhaps still are, those who think Calley

was a scapegoat. He was the only one of the twenty-six officers and enlisted men charged for crimes at My Lai to be convicted. Calley said he was only following orders.

Three days after the conviction, President Nixon reduced Calley's sentence to house arrest. He served three years before being freed in 1974 about the time Nixon was being impeached. Make of that what you will.

Calley eventually settled in Columbus and worked in the family jewelry business. He lived, by all accounts, an honorable life. Honorable but very private.

He spoke publicly about Vietnam and My Lai only once, to a small Columbus Kiwanis Cub in 2009: "There is not a day that goes by that I don't feel remorse for what happened that day at My Lai," he said. "I feel remorse for the Vietnamese who were killed, for their families, for the American soldiers involved and their families. I am very sorry."

As he spoke, his voice began to tremble.

I've thought a lot about William Calley, those days at the Grille, and Hugh Thompson over the years. I think about them when I am tempted to join the crowd and rush to judgment of a person or a situation.

I think about them and those words from First Corinthians: "It is as if I see through a glass darkly, what we now know in part, one day we will know in full."

Warrant Officer Hugh Thompson

Things That Last

We buried Sonny Dragoin last week, Thursday to be exact.

Good man, Sonny Dragoin. Saved my life once a long time ago, spring quarter, 1966, Beginning Swimming in the pool at old Alumni Gym, now long gone.

We were having some sort of a class race, and my team was in the middle of the pool. Somewhere in the deep end, I lost my confidence, my stroke rhythm, my whatever. I panicked, began furiously splashing around and going down fast.

Coach Dragoin held out his white rescue pole and yelled at me to grab it. As he was pulling me to the edge of the pool and safety, he let out one of his deep Sonny Dragoin belly laughs and said to the class—to me it seemed like to the world—"Look at that! Moby Dick, the great white whale …"

I'm not sure whether I laughed or got my feelings hurt, but we had a lot of fun with that story over the years after we had become friends. He loved to tell people how he saved my life.

When I was athletics director and going through some hard times, and there were many, he would remind me that he had saved my life, then add, "Now a lot of people wish I hadn't …"

He might have been kidding, or he might have been telling the truth. One never knew with Sonny.

Life was meant to be enjoyed, and he approached life with an ebullient sense of humor. He insisted others do the same. If you couldn't laugh, he thought, you were taking life—and yourself—too seriously.

As a student athlete, a wrestler, Anthony "Sonny" Dragoin served Auburn, his alma mater, his beloved alma mater, faithfully and well, as an assistant wrestling coach to the legendary "Swede" Umbach, as a PE instructor/professor, and as men's varsity golf coach.

His 1976 team won Auburn's first SEC golf championship. It was a grand and glorious day for Sonny and for Auburn.

Years later, the plaque that went with that championship led to one of the most poignant moments of my time in athletics.

It was '87 or '88. Someone had taken it upon themselves or had been assigned to reorganize and clean out the trophy cases in the coliseum to make way for bigger, more recent, more impressive trophies.

Sonny had been relieved of his golf-coaching responsibilities by then and worked full-time in the PE Department. He often walked down the hall to the Sports Information Office to visit and, more often than not, to remind the SID that he had once saved his life.

One day it was different. Instead of the usual jovial Sonny, he came in with tears in his eyes.

It's not easy to watch a grown man cry.

As he was walking down the hall by the door to the trophy case, he passed one of those big, movable, plastic institutional dumpsters. There, on top of the heap to be thrown away, was the plaque from his cherished and once celebrated golf championship.

With tears in his eyes and on his cheeks, he said, "I guess this doesn't matter anymore …"

It is the way of life, the old making way for the new. It is inevitable, but it still hurts if you are there to see it.

"Can I have this?" he asked, fighting back more tears.

Though I didn't have the authority to do it, I said, "Yes, take it …"

He clutched it to his chest as he walked down the hall, now unable to hold back the tears.

I thought about all of that last Thursday at Memorial Park.

"The boast of heraldry, the pomp of power and all that beauty and wealth ere gave," as Sir Thomas Gray wrote. None of it can stand up to the passage and ravages of time.

Buildings, anything of brick and mortar, streets, fields, lanes, drives, avenues and gardens, even trust funds will pass away. All things human pass away. Nothing of substance is eternal. The only things that last are what we do for others and what they in turn pass on to those who follow them. It is the natural order.

As I sat at the graveside Thursday and looked at those gathered there, family, friends, coworkers, former golfers, many of them with tears in their eyes, I thought about that truth that says, "A man's life is not measured by what he owns or by the abundance of his possessions."

And about Clarence, the angel, in *It's a Wonderful Life*, and about the conductor, the Tom Hanks character, in *Polar Express* when he told the little boy, "Any man who has friends is rich."

I hope Sonny Dragoin knew how rich he was.

Food for Thought

"How do we know what we really believe if we never truly look at it and get to know it in the light of challenge?"

That comes from Dr. Amanda L. Glaze-Crampes, a Christian biologist, in a recent opinion piece on AL.com, Alabama's major news outlet.

We need more of that kind of thinking.

Jesus even said to "love the Lord, thy God, with all thy heart, all thy soul, all thy mind, and all thy might." The Old Testament leaves out the word "mind," a significant omission.

If 'da man, Jesus, said use our minds, why don't we do it? Especially in matters of faith. Another case of selected hearing perhaps?

A faith, a belief system, is not yours until you have grappled with it and hammered it out on the red-hot anvil of thought, challenge, and experience.

If you still believe what your parents and your Sunday school teachers told you to believe, it's their faith, not yours. And if it's not your faith, it's like cast iron, brittle, and it will surely break when the trial and the testing comes. As they will surely come.

For a faith to last, for a faith to endure, it has to be your faith, not what somebody else told you to believe, but what you, *you*, truly believe and base your life upon.

An untested, unchallenged faith is no faith at all. Jesus said use our minds.

Why don't we do it?

Get in there, wrestle with it, grapple with it. Ask the hard questions. It forces you to be engaged with God, and God likes that. Very much.

Seek the truth—no matter where that truth may lead.

And fear not. You're only doing what Jesus said to do.

Remember?

Jiminy Cricket
"When You Wish upon a Star"
Pinocchio (the first politician?)

Snow White and the Seven Dwarfs
Doc, Grumpy, Happy, Sleepy, Bashful, Sneezy, Dopey
Prince Charming
How we dreamed of growing up and becoming Prince Charming
Some made it; most of us didn't

Peter Pan
Captain Hook
Smee
Wendy, Michael, and John
The Lost Boys
Tinkerbell

Howdy Doody
Lloyd Bridges

Seahunt
Buffalo Bob
Mighty Mouse, "Here I come to save the day …"
The Mickey Mouse Club

Davy Crockett
King of the Wild Frontier
Fess Parker
Buddy Ebsen
Mike Fink and the Great Keelboat Race
Coonskin caps
Sparklers

Zorro
The fox so cunning and free
Zorro, who makes the sign of the Z

Spin
Spin and Marty
Tim Considine
The Triple R

Clayton Moore
The Lone Ranger, daring and resourceful masked rider of the plains
A fiery horse with the speed of light, a cloud of dust, and hearty
Hi-Yo Silver! the Lone Ranger rides again
Tonto

Jay Silverheels
Scout
Merita Bread

George Reeves, TV's Superman
Faster than a speeding bullet, more powerful than a locomotive, able to leap tall buildings in a single bound. Look! Up in the sky! It's a bird! It's a plane. It's Superman ...
. ... who, disguised as Clark Kent, mild-mannered reporter for a great metropolitan newspaper, fought a never ending battle for truth, justice and the American way.

Roy Rogers and Trigger
Dale Evans and Buttermilk
Pat Buttram and Nellybelle
Gene Autry and Champion
Gabby Hayes
Smiley Burnett and
Frog Millhouse, one and the same

Wild Bill Hickok, Jingles
The Cisco Kid, Pancho
Hopalong Cassidy, who always ordered milk in the saloon. He was a good role model we were told, and we believed, at least for awhile
Lassie and Rin Tin Tin

Johnny Weissmuller's Tarzan
Johnny Sheffield, Bomba, Boy of the Jungle
Cheeta
Jane
Ramar of the Jungle

Bob Steele
Ward Bond
Wagon Train

Lash Larue
Allan "Rocky" Lane
Rex Allen
Randolph Scott
Johnny Mack Brown of Dothan and Alabama fame
Roy Barcroft, always the bad guy
Five-cent Coke and ten-cent popcorn

Or was it ten-cent Coke and five-cent popcorn?

Paladin
Have Gun Will Travel
Yancey Derringer, Pahoo
The Mavericks, Brett and Bart
Cheyenne, Sugarfoot, and Bronco Layne, tearing across the Texas plain

Shane
Old Yeller and, of course,
Annette Funicello

If you remember these, some or all of these, you had a good and happy childhood.

I know I did.

Word Pictures—
Pictures in Words

Ledes ...
The first sentence or paragraph of a news or feature story designed to catch the reader's attention and entice them to read on.

Grantland Rice, dean of American sportswriters, wrote what is considered to be the most famous lede ever written in the *New York Herald Tribune* on October 18, 1924:

> Outlined against a blue-gray October sky, the Four Horsemen rode again. In dramatic lore their names were Famine, Pestilence, Destruction and Death. These are only aliases. Their real names were Stuhldreher, Miller, Crowley and Layden. They formed the crest of the South Bend cyclone before which another fighting Army football team was swept over the precipice at the Polo Grounds yesterday

as 55,000 spectators peered down on the bewildering panorama spread on the green plain below.

A cyclone can't be snared. It may be surrounded but somewhere it breaks loose to keep on going. When the cyclone starts from South Bend, where the candle lights still gleam through the Indiana sycamores, those in the way must take the to the storm cellars at top speed.

Though not quite as flourishing as that (and few are), Auburn has had its share of great ledes. Here are but a few:

It was cold, clammy and uncomfortable.

A miserable sort of Saturday in Tennessee.

The clouds hung low over the perilous battleground which was Shields Watkins Field,

Gray Day, somber day, unhappy day for Tennessee.

For Auburn, it was something altogether different …

The sun was shining and the birds must have been singing and all of that.

Great day, wonderful day, happy for the team that came as an underdog and stayed to conquer. (Benny Marshall writing in the

Birmingham News on September 29, 1957, the day after Auburn stunned heavily favored and defending SEC champion Tennessee to begin its own march to the National Championship)

Marshall, the forever-dean of Alabama sportswriters, wrote another lede about another team and another game that still ranks as one of the greatest southern football ledes ever written. Though it was not about Auburn, it is a lede worth sharing for the beauty and drama of it:

> The score was 16–15.
>
> Numbers in lights on a scoreboard.
>
> Flip a switch, they are gone.
>
> But Alabama's Crimson Tide put them there Saturday at Grant Field and left them flaming for history.
>
> Wildly, magnificently, unbelievably, impossibly, Alabama came storming back from deep despair on this beautiful autumn afternoon and left Georgia Tech stunned … and beaten.
>
> For 30 minutes, this was Georgia Tech's field. Tech led 6–0, 9–0 and 15–0, and Alabama fought for its life.
>
> For 59 minutes, 59 seconds, this was Georgia Tech's football game.

> Then, all of a sudden, it was gone.
>
> They were beaten, but they wouldn't be. They were run out of Grant Field, but they came back.
>
> If the words are extravagant, so were they …

Who wouldn't want to read about that game? But we digress. Back to Auburn ledes:

Under the 1913 headline "Auburn's Tigers Come From Their Lair And Viciously Tear the Flesh of Dan McGugin's Commodores," James Chappell of the *Birmingham News* wrote:

> The lean, lank Tiger of the Plains, held back from its prey for twenty tedious years, feasts at last on the life-blood of the Commodores. Years of waiting had but added to the appetite until Saturday it was well-nigh insatiable. Even then the Commodores fought the Beast of the Jungle back, until battered, clawed, scratched, beaten, he succumbed to the deadly attack. Superior power had at last triumphed.

And in 1919 when Auburn won its final championship of the Mike Donahue era by capitalizing on two mistakes in the kicking game, a forty-five-yard return of a fumbled punt and a thirty-five-yard return of a blocked punt, to defeat Georgia

Tech 14–7 before 55,000 fans, the largest crowd ever to see a football game in the Deep South. John Heisman was the Tech coach. The next day, the *Birmingham News* read:

> Atlanta, Ga, Nov.26—Auburn has turned the old town upside down. The gilded youth from the Plains of Auburn celebrated all night and at an early hour this morning were still pounding the streets.
>
> Tech is in mourning and most of Atlanta's sporting circle is dead broke. Atlanta is far from being a happy place, for the Golden Tornado was converted into a light zephyr on Grant Field.

Upon the death of Mike Donahue, probably the best coach Auburn ever had, Ed Danforth of the *Atlanta Journal* wrote:

> You were nobody until you had beaten Auburn. That was the place card at the head of the table.

And in 1951, after Shug Jordan's first game as Auburn's coach, from Zipp Newman, sports editor of the *Birmingham News*:

> You can call 'em Tigers again and mean it …

Imagine the thrill of Auburn people in reading those words after an 0–10 season in 1950, which included a 41–0 shellacking at the hands of Vanderbilt. This time it was Auburn 24–Vanderbilt 14. A fifty-one-point turnaround in one year.

And there's always the great lines of the *News*'s Jerry Bryan in 1953 after Auburn had come from 21–0 behind in the fourth quarter to tie Mississippi State 21–21 in Starkville:

> Games like these come along only once in a long while. A team and its coach prove themselves great on the inside where the heart is. The public watches, understands and is proud.

Here are a few shorter ledes, sure to bring a smile to the hearts of Auburn people, those who were there and those who are reading these lines for the first time:

From Charles Land, the *Tuscaloosa News*, in 1970 after Auburn spotted Alabama a 17–0 first quarter lead but came back to win 33–28:

> Pat Sullivan may not be able to part the Red Sea, but he certainly has a way with Crimson Tides.

And Gary Sanders's opening lines, his lede lines, after Connie Frederick ran a fake punt eighty-four yards for Auburn's final touchdown in a resounding 49–26 victory over Alabama in 1969:

If you don't like to hear "War Eagle!" you're in for a rough night in Birmingham.

And finally:

Blindfolded, hands tied behind his back, Pat Sullivan would be a one-point favorite at his own execution.

Jack Doane, *Montgomery Advertiser*, wrote those words in September 1971 when Pat Sullivan led Auburn eighty-six yards in the last two minutes for a 10–9 victory over Tennessee in Knoxville in what some called "The Game of the Decade," the first of many "Game of the Decade" games.

We don't get that kind of writing anymore, and I for one miss it.

Do Animals Have Feelings?

People who say animals have no feelings use that as an excuse to treat animals any way they want to, usually cruelly.

Ode to the Green Wave ... And Why It Still Matters

Gordo beat Reform 53–8 last night.

After fifty-one years, why should it still matter?

But it does.

Fifty-one years since putting on that green jersey, walking down the sidewalk next to Mrs. Durrett's science room, the band playing, the Green Wave faithful murmuring in the distance in anticipation of what was to come, hearing and feeling the clack of those rubber cleats on the sidewalk, tension and expectation and maybe a little fear building with every step.

Fifty-one years, and it still matters.

I suppose it has to do with time and place. We are, all of us, the sum total of our experiences.

Reform, you see, is our archrival, our Alabama. "Re-form," as we called them—they preferred the much more haughty

PCHS: Pickens County High School—beat the Gordo of my youth nine years in a row. Remember how it felt when Alabama beat Auburn nine years in a row? That's how we felt about Reform.

Then, in 1957, John Meadows, destined to be a high school coaching legend in Alabama and Tennessee, came to coach at Gordo. The Green Wave rolled over Reform that year, 40–7. The next year, the Green Wave upset mighty, undefeated, top-ranked Reform 7–0 in the state high school game of the week, and the series has never been the same. Reform has won a few but not many.

Beating Reform is how we defined ourselves, kind of like Auburn beating Alabama or, God forbid, Alabama beating Auburn.

Five generations of Housels have played against Reform. Three generations, those of us who never lost to Reform, talk about it frequently; the other two generations, the generations who never beat Reform, seldom mention it. It still matters.

Why should it matter to me in 2015 that Auburn beat Georgia and Alabama the first games played, back in the 1890s? Why should it matter to me in 2015 that Auburn upset undefeated, top-ranked, Rose Bowl–bound Georgia 27–13 in 1942? Why should it matter to me that Auburn beat Georgia Tech 14–12 at Grant Field in 1955, breaking a fifteen-year losing streak to the Yellow Jackets?

Why should any of this matter to me in 2015? But it does.

It matters, I suppose, because of what the men of West Point call the "Long Gray Line," symbolic of a tradition that was present at West Point long before they came and will be present long after they are gone. But they are and will always be a part of that Long Gray Line, and they sense, they feel, a duty and an obligation to uphold its tradition.

Auburn people are like that. We care. And because we care, we have a sense of duty, a sense of obligation, and an appreciation for all that Auburn was, for all that Auburn is, and for all that Auburn will be long after our hour on the stage, as Mr. Shakespeare so aptly describes it, has come and gone. That's what caring is about. That's what loving Auburn is all about.

It has to do with time and place and the innate human desire to be a part of something bigger than we are and to leave that something better than we found it. For most, if not all, of us, that is Auburn.

The same is true, I suppose, with the Gordo Green Wave and that green jersey we wore so proudly, and, I hope, honorably so long ago.

"As they are now, so once were we; as we are now, so they shall be …"

Playing high school football, playing for the Green Wave, had a positive effect on my life. After all these years, it continues to have a positive effect. That's why we still care.

It is my hope, and the hope of all us old guys, that being part of the Green Wave tradition continues to have the same influence on young lives today as it had on ours.

And in years to come, when Coach Lolley, or whoever the coach may be, walks into the Gordo dressing room after the Reform game, quietly looks around, then asks, almost in a whisper, "What do you think about Reform?" the players of that day will be able to joyously shout the same two-word answer the players wearing green so resoundingly shouted last night. It was the right answer and the only acceptable answer.

Two words can say a lot. Especially at a time like that.

Last night around nine forty-five, Ole #82, Jerome Sullivan, an Alabama man, and Ole #22, Frank Elmore, a Troy man, called Ole #71, an Auburn man, to tell him that Gordo had beaten Reform. Ole #12, Larry Blakeney, knows by now.

All is right with the world at least for another year.

Gordo has beaten Reform.

Ode to the Green Wave ... And Why It Still Matters 49

The 1964 Gordo Green Wave
Gordo 58–Reform 0

What Fools We Be

Maybe ole Ben Franklin was right. Maybe the turkey should be our national emblem instead of the bald eagle.

At least it seems that way at election time. Rather than soaring like an eagle to our highest ideals, we revert to our lowest. Like turkeys, we root around the barnyard for whatever feed someone might throw our way, gobbling, gobbling, gobbling, trying to out-gobble the next fellow so we can be the biggest turkey of them all. Or so it seems.

It is true that the wild turkeys of which Franklin spoke are more majestic and smarter birds, but many lose their lives in pursuit of what they hope to be or consider to be pleasure. Turkeys have no sense of smell, as we, we the people, seem to have no sense of smell at the garbage and rot our elected leaders and those who would be our leaders feed us at election time.

It stinks to high heaven, but we, we the people, either ignore it or, sadly, believe it doesn't matter. Have we become the fools they think us to be and play us to be? It seems so.

It is insulting, it is embarrassing, and it is a desecration to the election process, supposedly the hallmark of our democracy.

Simply put, we the people have lost our way when we allow our leaders, and those who want to be our leaders, to pander to our anger, fears, frustration, and rage rather than to our hopes and dreams. Their campaigns encourage us to be our lesser selves rather than our better selves.

Case in point: Barack Obama.

We couldn't have an election in Alabama if it were not for Barrack Obama.

In the last three election cycles, virtually every politician in Alabama has run more "against Barack Obama" than against his or her opponent. "Against Obama." "Against Obama" is all we hear. "I'm against Obama more than my opponent is …"

It's okay to be opposed to the president—that's part of the political process—but isn't there something more? Must the chief criteria for holding office in Alabama be who can best bash Obama? It would appear there should be something more.

Anti-Obamaism has even filtered down to state and local elections. Two years ago, one candidate for state senate went so far as to Photoshop a picture of his opponent with Obama at Toomer's Corner. Obama at Toomer's Corner? What kind of fools do they think we are? Barack Obama has never been anywhere in Lee County. A normally good man sinking to a new low to win an election.

Not to burst anyone's bubble or bruise anyone's political ego, but President Obama, respect him or abhor him, couldn't care less about who holds Alabama House seat 79, Senate seat 27, or any other legislative seat in Alabama. He has, or should have, more important things on his mind than who wins a legislative race in Alabama.

And Barack Obama, love him or loathe him, cares even less about who serves on the Auburn City Council or the Lee County Commission.

But you wouldn't know that at election time. One would think, or be led to believe, that a whole wing of the White House has been set aside for the express purpose of defeating a particular candidate in a particular Alabama political race, even the city council and county commission.

It is absurd. It is ridiculous. And yet our politicians, our supposed leaders, put that trash, that rot, at our feet and expect us to believe it. And apparently we do. Isn't there something more, something better?

And this matter of liberals and conservatives.

What does it mean to be a liberal? What does it mean to be a conservative?

We no longer know. Perhaps we no longer care. We define those words, those terms, only by whether or not someone agrees or disagrees with us.

We call someone a liberal, a dirty word in Alabama, when he or she doesn't agree with us. Someone who does agree with us is a conservative, a great Alabamian and a great American. The same is true in the opposite direction. We use labels to define and denigrate our fellow citizens. That's not good. That's simple-minded.

We've lost our common ground. Rather than come together and have reasonable discussions, we come together to gobble, gobble, call each other names, and hurl insults and labels at one another, like a bunch of turkeys.

We live in a political world reminiscent of trench warfare in World War I. No-man's-land, the land between the two trenches, was the worst place to be. You got shot at by everybody.

But isn't that where we should be, where we ought to be? In no-man's-land between the armed and warlike camps of liberals and conservatives who can't define themselves except in terms of opposition to one another.

We should be in that middle ground because, truth be told, there's a degree of liberalism and conservatism in all of us. On some issues, we lean to the liberal side, on others to the conservative side.

Could we be talking about the great silent majority? If so, it's time for that great silent majority to stand up, to speak up, and to demand more from our leaders than we are getting.

Lord, O Lord, send us leaders, leaders who will lead us from the swamp of angst, fear, and anger, the absolutes of where we are, to higher ground where we can have free, open, and respectful discussions about who we are as a people and where we, as a state and a nation, can and ought to be.

May we prove Ben Franklin wrong and those who wanted the eagle right ...

But we've got some work to do.

Worth Thinking about on a Sunday Afternoon

Religion is at its best when it forces us to ask hard questions of ourselves. It is at its worst when it deludes us into thinking we have all the answers for everybody else.

—Archibald MacLeish

Friendship, a Puppy, a Lasting Legacy

You have read about, heard about, and talked about the many ways Auburn's and Georgia's athletic success seem intertwined, almost interrelated.

Pat Dye, Vince Dooley, Shug Jordan, Joel Eaves, Gene Lorendo, Steve Greer, Steve Dennis, Stacy Searels, Erk Russell, Lee Hayley, Kermit Perry, Mike Hubbard, Alan Thomas, Ben Beaty, Jason Peevy, and now Will Muschamp and Rodney Garner. There are many more. All good Georgia or Auburn men who went to one school, then moved to the other to help it find success.

Claude Felton, the best Georgia man I know, referred to the ties between Auburn and Georgia as "the Underground Railroad," leading from Auburn to Athens sometimes and from Athens to Auburn at other times.

To an outsider, "War-Dog" or "Bull-Eagle" might seem an appropriate cheer for this game. The ties between Auburn and Georgia, the South's oldest rivals, are that close, that intertwined.

A little known but perhaps most interesting and lasting tie between the two schools involves Uga, the Georgia Bulldog mascot. The first Uga, Uga I, was an Auburn dog before he became a Georgia Dawg.

Here's the story as told by Sonny Seiler, owner, lover, caretaker, and keeper of all the Ugas who have come to represent Georgia football's highest and finest ideals of fight, courage, and tenacity.

You may know Sonny, or know of Sonny. He was the "country lawyer" from Savannah who successfully defended Jim Williams in his murder trial in the best-selling book *Midnight in the Garden of Good and Evil*. In a reversal of roles, he portrayed the judge in the movie version.

He can also be seen in *The Legend of Bagger Vance* as the guest who comes to dinner at the boarding house and visits with legendary sportswriter Grantland Rice, who, in real life, penned the most famous football lede in the history of the game, "Outlined against a blue-gray October sky, the Four Horseman rode again …" That lede, that Grantland Rice.

But back to Sonny, Uga, and an Auburn Man, Frank Heard of Columbus, Georgia.

Out of his friendship with Seiler, and with deep respect for his friend's great love of the University of Georgia, Heard gave Seiler a pure white English bulldog puppy in the early fifties. That puppy was to become the first Uga, Uga I, in

1956. All Ugas have descended from that one Dawg, that one gift, Uga I.

Uga IX, who goes by the given name Russ, will be retired at next week's Georgia–Georgia Southern game in Athens. It seems fitting and proper that Uga IX's last road trip is to Auburn.

A gift from an Auburn Man to a Georgia Man, a lasting legacy of friendship between two men, two great institutions, and two great athletic programs.

That's the way it should be.

Enjoy your retirement, Russ. You have served the Bulldogs well. Sonny and Frank, the Georgia Man and the Auburn Man, are proud.

A Christmas Eve Epiphany

It was a long time ago, now, back in the days when I thought I knew all the answers, when, in reality, I didn't have any idea about what the questions were, back in my college days, maybe a little later.

Back in the days when I had to slip a bottle of Jack Daniel's into my parents' house if I was going to have that little midnight toddy to which I had become accustomed because I thought it was cool.

I was sitting alone in the den that Christmas Eve night, in the big easy chair, drink in hand, sipping my Jack Daniel's and running the TV channels trying find something, anything, to watch as Christmas Eve turned ever so slowly into Christmas Day.

Maybe it was the liquor, maybe not, but suddenly I had a feeling I had never had before. It was, and continues to be, the closest thing to an epiphany I've ever experienced. It was the assurance, the realization, the trust that what I wanted so desperately to believe true was, indeed, true.

On the television screen was a Christmas Mass from the Vatican in the heart of Rome. In Rome, capital of the empire that killed Jesus, they now celebrate his birth.

Two thousand years before, the Romans crucified Jesus because he was said to be King of kings and Lord of lords.

Now, two thousand years later, descendants of those who crucified him celebrate his birth, and now they, too, proclaim him Lord and King.

Celebrating the birth of Jesus, in the heart of Rome, capital of the empire that killed him.

The place that was once the antithesis of Christianity is now the center of the faith.

That is no small thing.

It speaks of darkness and light.

A light that two thousand years of darkness has not been able to overcome.

A light that promises ultimate triumph.

The light of Christmas …

Rhett Butler and the Auburn Tigers

As we have limped toward what appeared to be a merciful end to a disappointing football season, I have been reminded time and again of a scene from *Gone with the Wind*.

The Yankees have come, and Atlanta is burning. Rhett and Scarlett, with Melanie, Prissy, and the baby in the back of the wagon, have made their way through the flames of the burning warehouse district and exploding ammunition train cars, fought off an attack by hooligans and scavengers—real bad guys—and are now on a rutted, heavily traveled dirt road leading away from the defeated and burning city.

The fires of Atlanta light the sky behind them with a bright orange glow. Around their wagon walk the ragged remnants of the once-proud Confederate Army, now battered, bruised. Beaten.

"Look at them," Rhett says with anguish in his voice. "They were going to whip the Yankees in a month."

Against the continuing backdrop of the burning Atlanta,

the sounds of death and dying around them, Rhett, Scarlett, and the others drive on. They cross a bridge and come to the inevitable fork in the road.

To the right lies the road to Tara; to the left lies a road of uncertainty, seemingly filled with even more defeat and despair. That is the direction in which the wounded, struggling soldiers move.

Rhett climbs down from the wagon, hands the reins of the horse to Scarlett, and says, "This is where I leave you …"

"What are you doing?" Scarlett asks in her condescending way. "Where are you going?"

To which Rhett replies, "I'm going to join the army, my dear, to join our brave lads in gray …"

"You've got to be joking," Scarlett says, as only Scarlett could say it. "They are running away. They won't fight anymore. You will get yourself killed …"

"Oh, they'll turn and make a stand," Rhett says, "and when they do, I'll be with them …"

So it has been with Auburn football this year. And so it is with us, you, me, all of us.

This was supposed to be our year, our time to shine. We, too, were going the whip the Yankees, in twelve weeks, three short months. We began the campaign ranked sixth in the nation with dreams of going higher, perhaps even to the ultimate prize, the national championship. To some, the SEC Championship was a given. This was to be our year …

But it was not to be. For whatever reason, and there could be many reasons, it was not to be.

But Auburn, our Auburn Tigers, will make a stand.

Next week, next month, next year, they will make a stand, they will turn, and they will fight.

And when they do, like Rhett Butler, we'll be with them.

Rhett says goodbye to Scarlett at the turn for Tara.

Even Beating Alabama Has Its Limits

Beating Alabama does have its limits, as Bruce Pearl learned this week, the morning after he got his first win over Alabama as Auburn's head basketball coach.

Bruce went be-bopping into Chappy's Deli on Dean Road, a name you are familiar with if you visit this site often, with one of his best friends from his days at Tennessee.

He knew, having found out the hard way, that the back booth at Chappy's is reserved for one of the world's erstwhile coffee and breakfast clubs, unnamed but no less erstwhile. It is the site from which many of these columns and essays often spring.

Early in his time at Auburn, Coach Pearl and Johnny Kincey, one of his closest Auburn friends and confidants, unknowingly and innocently sat down in the back booth at Chappy's. They were firmly but politely asked to find another booth or table, that this one was reserved, even though there was no sign or marking on the table, only an upturned chair.

Courtney Cox, who oversees the servers at Chappy's, felt bad about asking Auburn's brand-new basketball coach to move, but if Courtney is anything, she is loyal to her regulars.

Coach Pearl and Johnny were surprised and taken aback, but when the back booth guys arrived, everyone had a big laugh about it. They were quickly invited to join us in the back booth but respectfully declined.

"I've got to earn the right to sit there," Pearl said, laughing as only he can laugh. "When we make it to the tournament, I will have earned the right to sit there, and I will gladly take my seat …"

Everybody laughed again, but the new coach was quickly corrected. Getting to the NCAA tournament may be the goal of every college basketball team in America, but at Auburn, there was something else too: beating Alabama.

"Beat Alabama twice in the same year," he was told, "here and in Tuscaloosa, and you can sit here anytime you want to. We might even give you the booth!"

With Auburn's 83–77 win Tuesday night, he was halfway there.

Then came Wednesday morning.

On a morning that should have been reserved for celebrating and basking in the glow of what may have been his best, if not his greatest, victory at Auburn (Kentucky has that spot), Coach Pearl came to Chappy's again.

He avoided the back booth, tapping it as he walked by and saying as he always does, with a smile, "One day, one day …"

He and his friend sat down at the back table—not the back booth but the back table. Just as they were settling in, the always efficient Courtney walked up and said, "Coach, I hate to do this to you again, but this is Wednesday, and Dr. McLaughlin (Wayne), Jack Simms, and the Turners (Karen and Homer) sit here every Wednesday. I'm going to have to ask you to move again."

Chappy's, you see, is somewhat like TV's *Cheers* bar, a place where everybody knows your name—and your place. It's one of the places that make Auburn "Auburn." Church pews are not the only semireserved spots in the South, and apparently, beating Alabama only goes so far.

"I really hated to ask him to move again," Courtney said, "especially after his first win over Alabama, but that's where Dr. McLaughlin, Jack, and the Turners sit."

Later, as I walked by his new and now acceptable booth, I congratulated Coach Pearl on his victory and told him what another coach a long time ago said after his first win over Alabama.

Running into the dressing room after his victory, the coach, who shall go unnamed, shouted, "Now I'm an Auburn Man. I beat Alabama ..."

Coach Pearl, to his everlasting credit, looked incredulous at the thought.

"There's a lot more to being an Auburn Man than beating Alabama," he said, shaking his head. "Auburn is a special place, and that specialness is more important than beating Alabama. Beating Alabama is fun, but there is far more to Auburn than just beating Alabama …"

With a perspective like that, Bruce Pearl is welcome in the back booth at Chappy's at any time. Anytime.

He understands. He gets it.

He's an Auburn Man.

Coach Bruce Pearl and David Housel celebrate sweep of Alabama.

Shades of Green—
The Masters

Words do not allow me to say how I feel about the Masters. It is a matter of heart and of soul, far beyond likes and dislikes, far beyond the ability of mere human words to convey.

For the rest of my life, forevermore, a part of my heart and a part of my soul will be in Augusta at the end of the first full week in April. In Augusta. At the Augusta National. At the Masters. The Masters.

It wasn't always this way. I remember my first Masters in 1975. It was raining that Thursday during the opening round. During a suspension of play, I stood under a tree wearing a borrowed raincoat. *What am I doing here?* I thought. *If I ever get out of here, I'm never coming back. Never.*

Then the sun came out and changed my life forever.

It is difficult to describe or explain my love affair with the Masters. All the words have been said, and they come up short. They are all inadequate.

"Cathedral in the Pines," "Amen Corner," "Golf's Holy Ground," even "A Tradition Unlike any Other …" All inadequate.

It's more beautiful and greener than one can imagine, shades of green everywhere, shades of green. Every hole is named for a flower, and that flower graces that hole. With azaleas everywhere, it is beautiful beyond compare, beautiful beyond belief. A little bit of the beauty of heaven right here on earth, right now. Not a blade of grass out of place.

Hundreds, thousands of people so quiet you can hear the click of the putter hitting the ball. And if it is good, if it goes in, goes in the hole, there arises a cheer that is heard from Augusta to Aiken, to Martinez and beyond, maybe, it seems, all the way to Atlanta.

I was blessed—honored, really—to attend thirty-nine straight Masters, starting in 1975, the year Jack Nicklaus, the Golden Bear, beat Johnny Miller and Tom Weiskopf with that long, snaky putt at 16, through 2013.

My legs and feet finally gave out, and I can no longer walk those hallowed hills of green or meander down to Amen Corner where the water in Rae's Creek slowly makes its way through golf's most beautiful setting. My legs and feet may not be what they used to be, but that has not affected my heart, my mind, or my soul. I remember, and I am grateful for the opportunity to have been there.

Some of my greatest memories have come at the Masters:

I've seen the Big Three, Palmer, Nicklaus, and Player, in their prime, seen them as they aged and moved slowly into retirement except for the ceremonial first tee shots that officially open the tournament every year. This year, for the first time, Arnie is not able to participate in that most moving of ceremonies. There was nothing better, nothing more exciting, than seeing Jack and Arnie paired together, going head to head in their prime. Phil vs. Tiger? Not even close.

I saw Lee Elder, the first black to play in the Masters, hit his first shot. I saw Tom Watson, Ben Crenshaw, and now, perhaps, Tiger Woods come as young men, saw them become champions, then begin the long, slow fade that comes not from a club but with time and age. Old champions, like old soldiers, never die; they just fade away. I have been honored to watch them and many others in their prime and now I fade away with them.

As always, a new generation has come forth to challenge Augusta's hallowed fairways and greens. Jordan Spieth, Jason Day, Rory McIlroy, Adam Scott, and, hopefully, Jason Dufner will have their moment in the sun, their one great hour upon the stage, then fade away, as all before them have faded away. Only the Masters will remain.

But if they should be fortunate enough to win the Green Jacket, as Spieth and Scott have done, they will forevermore be part of a tradition that is, as Jim Nance says, unlike any other.

The Masters, why do I love it so?

It's history and tradition. It is the only major to be played at the same place every year. Memory lives here. Memories of great shots, great accomplishment, great disappointment, heartbreak and sorrow, many warm memories of spring afternoons spent with friends, enjoying golf, a beer, a cold beer, and a ham and cheese on rye.

It is the pride and appreciation of those who attend the tournament, the patrons as they are called, who, if they see a piece of paper on the ground—which is not often—will pick it up and put it in their pocket until they find a trash bag. The patrons understand and appreciate the aura and majesty of this place, this Cathedral in the Pines. Imagine seeing that at Jordan-Hare or Bryant-Denny Stadium. You won't, and you never will.

The lack of commercialism. No corporate logos, not one, add to the ambiance and sanctity of the event and the location. There is no place for crass commercialism here. All concessions are reasonably priced, almost given away, by standards of other major sporting events, even college football.

The fact that members of "The National," as Augustans call the host club, make you feel so welcome. "Thank you for coming," they say as you enter. "We hope you have a good day at the Masters." And on leaving, they are there again: "We hope you had a good day at the Masters. We hope you will come back again ..." And we always do, or at least want to.

Those men—and now women—in the green coats. I want to thank them, and on occasion have thanked them, for being the sentinels and guardians for all that is good about the game of golf.

Bobby Jones, founder of the Masters and Augusta National, and its President in Perpetuity, would be proud. Very proud.

So would Clifford Roberts, who was with Jones in his every endeavor and served as enforcer of rules, regulations, and, most importantly, the traditions of Augusta National and the Masters. Jones was the good guy, Roberts the heavy, and golf owes them both a debt that can never be repaid.

No cell phones are allowed on the grounds, and therein may lie part of my great love and affection for the Masters. In my working days, no one could bother me here. The world, even the problems and challenges of Auburn (and they could be many), could not intrude on my place of escape, release, and solitude. For four days every April, this was my sanctuary.

A week ago in this space, we talked about changes that come with the seasons of our lives and the need to accept and embrace them. The time has come for me to accept and embrace those changes in my life.

At the urging of friends better than I or anyone deserve to have, after a two-year absence, I am going back to my sanctuary in the pines, back to Augusta, back to the Masters.

I can no longer walk those sacred hills as I once did, but I am going back, doing something I once swore I would never do: swallow my pride and ride a scooter.

Yes, there is some apprehension involved, but I'm prepared. I've been to Publix, practiced driving a scooter, didn't hit any aisles or knock over any displays, so I am ready to go. Ready and eager to go:

Back to the Masters.

Back to my spiritual home.

Back to my sanctuary.

To see and experience those shades of green once again.

The Day After

It's a story two thousand years old and as modern as today and tomorrow. It is Palm Sunday, and it is our story.

On that first Palm Sunday long ago, people, people like us, like you and me, lined the streets, waved palm branches, and shouted their hosannas.

But where were they five days later when Pilate stood before them and asked, "Who shall I free, Jesus or Barabbas?" Some, perhaps many, of these same people, the same people who were waving psalm branches on Sunday, now shouted, "Barabbas ... Barabbas ... Give us Barabbas."

Before we condemn them too harshly, let us think about ourselves today, on this Palm Sunday. Today, we, too, come together to sing our praises, shout our hosannas, and say our amens.

But what will we do tomorrow, the next day, and the day after that? Will we do the same thing they did?

Will our thoughts, words, and deeds, the way we live our lives, say, "Give us Jesus," or will the lives we lead shout once again, as they did, "Barabbas, Barabbas ... Give us Barabbas ..."?

Are we really that different from them?

Jesus or Barabbas?

Who will it be?

Not today. We all know what we would say today.

But what will we say, what will our lives say, tomorrow?

Tomorrow is when it counts.

Jesus or Barabbas?

Mother's Day

It will soon be Mother's Day, a good time to think not only of our mothers but of other women who impacted our lives and made us, for better or worse, the person we are today.

Here are some of the women who, in addition to my mother, have affected my life down through the years, as Coach Jordan would say.

I, as most men, would have to start with my wife. There is no way I can explain what she means to me. I am a better man, a much better man, because of her. I love her for that and for so much more.

The day she said yes to yet another of my many proposals, September 29, 1984, just after Auburn had beaten Tennessee 29–10 here in Auburn, was and remains the greatest day of my life, and it has nothing to do with beating Tennessee. The most meaningful parts of my life started that day. I can't imagine life without Susan. I never want to.

Neither could I imagine my life without "Hat-T," Hattie Mae Blair, the African American woman who raised me in the same manner my mother did. When Momma left for school in the morning—she taught elementary school for thirty-eight years and had class sizes ranging from less than ten to more than forty—Hat-T was always there. I don't remember a time in my early life without Momma or Hat-T being there for me.

When I cried, she hugged me. When I stubbed my toe, cut my finger, or scraped my knee, she put mercurochrome on it. When I had a question, I went to her. When I had a problem, I went to her. When I was lonesome, I went to her.

Yes, I appreciated then and appreciate even more now those home-cooked meals she put on the table every Monday through Friday at 11:30. We called it dinner then; today it's known as lunch. But more than anything, I loved and appreciated her because she loved me, hugged me, and cared about me. That she was black never mattered. No matter how old I got, I was always her "Baby," and she was always my "Hat-T."

I shall never forget the last time I saw her. On the way to Starkville for a Mississippi State game, I stopped by the nursing home in Reform to see her. The years had not been good to her. She had lost her husband, Ed, and two of her three children.

Her final days were spent in an almost comatose state. I knew she probably wouldn't know me, but I went anyway. How could I not go? I entered her room, sat by her bed, and held her hand. I talked to her, but she gave no indication she heard or even knew I was there.

When the time came to go, knowing it would probably be the last time I would ever see her, I leaned down, kissed her on the forehead, and said, "I love you, Hat-T." As I turned to leave, she opened her eyes, just for a moment, and said, as best she could in her condition, "I uv oou."

As I write these words, tears flow down my cheeks as freely as they did on that day. I am a blessed man to have had Hat-T in my life. Truly blessed.

There are other life blessings too:

Miss Winnie Elmore, the sweetest, kindest kindergarten Sunday school teacher any child could ever have; Miss Pauline Pate who had the patience of Job when dealing with an unruly first-grade class back in 1953; Miss Mary Price, second-grade teacher, the closest thing to a saint I've ever known; and "Miz" Sherrill, who always had time to listen.

Mrs. Ruth Junkin, who encouraged my love of reading by letting me check books out of the school library in the summer; Nina Reeves, the loving heart and soul of Camp Sumatanga, a Methodist church camp in north Alabama; Hazel Mullenix, who taught me to appreciate literature and to overcome the inevitable anxiety of leaving home for college, even to my beloved Auburn.

Dorothy Durrett—Mrs. Durrett—one of the first female high school principals in Alabama. She was tough, she was stern, she was good, and she was fair. No matter how mad or irritated she might get, you always knew she loved you.

She was and still is the best example of tough love I've ever known.

Blanche Britt, my Auburn mother in every way; Mary Virginia Moore in the Speech Department at Auburn, who demonstrated her care again and again in my college years and continues to do so today; Mrs. Evelyn Jordan, Coach Jordan's wife, who saw something in me others did not; and my Baptist friends Helen Brown and Jo Randle. Both have lived lives of conviction, courage, and commitment, Helen as a white teacher in Tuskegee during the early days of the civil rights era, Jo as a missionary to Japan. Both continue to demonstrate God's love every day.

Jane Moore, that "wun-da-ful woman," as Horace Vandergelder in *Hello, Dolly!* would have called her had he been fortunate enough to know her. She is wise, smart, loving, and kind, always finding a way to make you laugh, smile, and feel good about yourself. But, like Dolly Levi Gallagher, also from *Hello, Dolly!*, she has a tough, disciplined side. To know her is to love her, and to love her is to be inspired by her. She is a gift.

Sarah Goolsby, at Auburn United Methodist Church, who reassures me that it is okay to think about, even question, our faith because until we question it, until we determine what we ourselves believe, it's not our faith; it's only the faith of someone else trying to tell us what to believe. That kind of faith won't hold when the storms come, as they inevitably will.

We must make our faith our own. Sarah Goolsby, an angel of wisdom and perspective.

The purpose of this piece is not so much to tell you about the women who have influenced my life as it is to encourage you to think about the women who have influenced your life and to suggest, even urge, you to reach out and tell them they mattered. And they continue to matter.

Yes, it all starts with our mothers—our mommas—but there are many more women to think about and be grateful for on this Mother's Day.

So many more.

Where would we be, who would we be, without their influence in our lives?

Hattie Mae Blair, "Hat-T," with a very young James Raymond Housel

It's Okay to Get Mad at God

For many years, for most of my life really, I avoided reading the Psalms—those messy, gooey God-is-great-God-is-good psalms.

Or so I thought …

Then, in Disciple Bible study, I began to read the Psalms, really read the Psalms, and they were totally different than I expected.

Yes, there were the syrupy God-is-great-God-is-good" psalms, but there was much more, psalms of anger, psalms of frustration, palms of fear, hope, and lament, the whole range of human emotions, often raw and bleeding emotion. Sometimes, when we really read the Psalms, we may cringe at just how honest the psalmists were in their prayers and conversations with God.

All of which is to say that God can handle our anger and frustration. After all, God is God, and He is a great God, a God of love and a God of grace. It's okay to get mad at God and to question Him. He is a big God. He can handle it.

If the Psalms do nothing else, they let us know that it is okay to be honest with God and freely share the wide range of emotions we as humans have. He created us, and He already knows our hopes, fears, and frustrations, even if we ourselves won't articulate them.

Ain't No More Iron Bowl

Enough of all this talk about the Iron Bowl.

Iron Bowl this; Iron Bowl that; Iron Bowl infinitum.

There hasn't been an Iron Bowl since 1987. That's the last time the crowd at Legion Field in Birmingham was divided about evenly. It never was truly a half-and-half split because most of Legion Field's several thousand bondholders were Alabama fans. But it was close enough not to quibble about it. Not now.

When Alabama's Sam Bailey proposed a change in the fifty-fifty ticket split in 1988, the Iron Bowl was doomed. Alabama needed more tickets to the Auburn game to get its fledgling Tide Pride program rolling. Auburn, of course, was only too happy to oblige. Auburn had wanted to move its home game with Alabama to Auburn for many years, but the ticket split had always been a thorny issue. Now, at Alabama's initiative, that issue was settled.

Auburn (Athletics Director Pat Dye) quickly agreed to Alabama's proposal that the visiting team receive 10,500 tickets, with the rest going to the home team. The fifty-fifty split was gone; the Iron Bowl as we knew it was gone. The game was headed to Auburn and, eventually, to Tuscaloosa.

Call it what you will, the Auburn-Alabama game or the Alabama-Auburn game, but don't call it the Iron Bowl. There ain't no more Iron Bowls.

When the game was played in Birmingham, the name "Iron Bowl" was appropriate. Birmingham, "the Pittsburgh of the South" as it was called, was one of only two, maybe three, places in the entire country where all of the materials needed to make steel—coal, iron ore, and limestone—were found in the same location. In addition to being called the "Magic City," Birmingham was also known as the "Steel City." And rightly so.

Iron, in those days, was an appropriate metaphor for the intensity of this rivalry. Both teams, Auburn and Alabama, often displayed iron will and strength in claiming that most cherished prize, "Braggin' Rights," as Coach Bryant called it, for an entire year.

Those were the days. As Coach Dye observed, every play was a big play for one side or the other. No matter what happened, a three-yard gain or a three-yard loss, one side of the stadium, forty thousand or so, cheered. There was never a quiet moment in those kinds of Iron Bowls. They were quite special.

Even the crowds outside the stadium were special. Split half and half, old-school emotion and pride were very much evident in the mixing and mingling of fans that today's crowds, overwhelmingly dominated by fans of the home team, do not have.

This is not a plea to go back to Birmingham; no, nothing like that. It has been good for Auburn and good for Alabama, maybe better for Alabama, to have the game on campus, but campus games, however big they may be, do not have the same sense of tingling excitement and anticipation the old Iron Bowls had.

The Iron Bowl used to be a spectacle, both bands on the field at the same time playing the national anthem, both sides, about evenly divided, cheering vociferously for their team. It was a mutual celebration of all that was good about football in the state of Alabama. That was the Iron Bowl. Now that spectacle, that celebration, is gone. Gone forever.

Yet the misnomer "Iron Bowl" has persisted, used today by the media and encouraged by licensing companies eager to use the term "Iron Bowl" to make a buck or two more.

It has persisted to the point of the ridiculous. Now we have not only the football Iron Bowl, we have Iron Bowl of men's basketball, the Iron Bowl of women's basketball, the Iron Bowl of gymnastics, the Iron Bowl of baseball and softball, the Iron Bowl of soccer, the Iron Bowl of track, tennis, swimming, and golf. Maybe more.

Yes, teams from Auburn and Alabama ought to play in every sport every year—it is a special rivalry—but just because they play doesn't make it an Iron Bowl.

The Iron Bowl of swimming and diving? Somebody needs to use some common sense.

"It's a freaking marketing tool," said one person familiar with the intricacies of collegiate licensing. "It's all about money."

About 8.5 percent is added to the cost of every product bearing the term "Iron Bowl" or using the Iron Bowl logo. Thus, a product that would normally sell for twenty dollars would now cost about two dollars more, and that cost would be passed on to you, the consumer.

"There isn't any iron made in Lee County," he continues, "or in Tuscaloosa for that matter. Yet we still call it the Iron Bowl. Why?"

An argument could be made, weak though it is, that bowl games do not have to be played in the cities where they originated in order to maintain their original and traditional names. The Rose and Sugar Bowls could be cited as examples.

There is a difference, however, in playing the Rose Bowl at Duke in 1942 because of fear the Japanese might attack a large gathering of people on the West Coast, and playing the Sugar Bowl in Atlanta in 2006 because of the havoc wreaked in New Orleans by Hurricane Katrina. A big difference.

Lest you think this is just another Auburn man's rant against Birmingham, two of the best Alabama men I know, noted New York author Allen Barra and beloved Alabama quarterback Scott Hunter, share the same view: "If the game is not played in Birmingham, it shouldn't be called the Iron Bowl." That has been Scott's position since 1989. And as Allen notes, "There hasn't been an iron industry in Birmingham in years."

Note that, in spite of our marked differences in football allegiances, on this point we are united. Strongly and firmly united.

But we are also realistic. "Iron Bowl" has gone corporate. It is a way to make more money, piddling though it may be, and there is no way of going back. "The Iron Bowl," most likely, is with us forever.

But that doesn't keep the three of us, and perhaps others, from being voices in the wilderness.

> If the game's not played in Birmingham, it shouldn't be called the Iron Bowl …
>
> If the game's not played in Birmingham, it shouldn't be called the Iron Bowl …
>
> There ain't no more Iron Bowls! Damnit!

Voices crying in the wilderness.

But we still cry.

Muhammad Ali

Muhammad Ali was a great American.

Many, perhaps many, many, of my generation would beg to differ, perhaps strongly, questioning his conversion to Islam and the sincerity of his claim to be a conscientious objector.

Ali, of course, refused to be drafted during the Vietnam War. He said he could not support that war or any war. It was against his religion and his faith—when that faith is properly read, interpreted, and followed. Life, he believed, was too precious to destroy.

Why is he a great American?

He is a great American because rather than running away, rather than go to Canada as many of his generation did, he chose to fight for his convictions in the courts and legal system of his country and trust it to decide his fate.

If we are a nation of law. We have to respect its laws and realize they are for everyone, not just those with whom we agree.

Ultimately, the Supreme Court sided with Ali.

Though he had many great victories, that may have been the greatest victory of all.

He made our country stronger by forcing it to examine its core beliefs and values. Were we really a nation of law, of freedom of religion, of freedom of speech, a nation where a man's conscience could be his guide? Were we what we claimed to be, or were we something else? Something less? Muhammad Ali helped us decide.

I didn't always see the issue this way, but as I aged and began to think more about it, the more I grew to appreciate Muhammad Ali and to realize how truly great he was, outside the ring as well as in. And I have grown to admire and respect him more and more as the years have gone by.

A man can serve his country in many ways. Ali served his by forcing it to examine itself.

He became an ambassador for peace, goodwill, even love the world over.

He has proven himself to be the man he claimed to be so long ago.

Father's Day

My father, David A. (for Alpheus) Housel is the greatest man I have ever known, a man of integrity and honor, ramrod straight when it came to right and wrong.

His father, Alpheus Housel, died when he was seventeen, and Daddy never had a chance to go to college. He never complained. He did what he had to do, entering the family hardware business in 1931 and, except for World War II, spending the rest of his life working in Housel Hardware, from 1931 until he died in 1990, fifty-nine years in all.

He was a member of what Tom Brokaw calls "The Greatest Generation." It is an apt term. He fought with George Patton's Seventh Armored Division and was in the thick of the Battle of the Bulge, fighting for all he was worth at St. Vith. He was awarded the Bronze Star when he led his outfit to safety after being surrounded by the Germans.

As with most soldiers who fought in World War II, he never talked about it. It was too terrible, too horrible, to relive again, even in memory.

Daddy was and remains the primary influence in my life,

but there were others too. Some of them you will know, some you won't, but they all contributed to making me the man I am today and the better man I yet hope to be in years to come. Here are some of them:

Leonard, Ralph, and Raymond Housel, my uncles. Starting in 1958, Uncle Raymond, one of Auburn's first season ticket holders, would send me football programs rolled up in a single envelope after each home game. I still have them.

"Mr. Marvin" Price, the druggist who lived across the street in Gordo and introduced me at an early age to the loyalty needed to be an Auburn Man, especially in the hard times.

My high school coaches, Tommy White and Pete Steele, who helped me find a toughness and determination I didn't know I had. Larry Blakeney, Frank Elmore, and Jerome Sullivan, the Alabama man, friends then, friends now, steadfast friends forever. Raymond, my brother.

Coach Jordan, Coach Beard, Bill Beckwith, Buddy Davidson, and Kenny Howard. They sensed my love of Auburn and enabled me to realize my greatest and only dream: to be a part of Auburn.

Oxford Stroud, who freed me to write. Words, he said in that Advanced Comp class so long ago, were meant to communicate, not to follow rules of grammar. That may be the greatest single thing I learned at Auburn. It changed my life.

Paul C. Burnett and Mickey Logue, our journalism professors. They helped our generation of journalism students be better than we could have ever been without their guidance, instruction, care, and encouragement. Behind his back, we called Mr. Burnett "P.C."—P.C. for "Pole Cat"—but we admired and respected him. We think he knew about the nickname—so our respect.

Mike Warren, for being a friend when I needed a friend.

Clarke Stallworth, city editor of the *Birmingham News*, who believed in me and gave me a chance. I shall forever be indebted to him.

Bob Ingram, the best political writer and commentator this state and perhaps the South has ever known. How I admired and respected him. I wanted to make a difference as he made a difference.

The men who kept—and keep—me on the path of the straight and narrow and on the path of grace: E.L. McFee, O.C. Brown, John Jeffers, Tim Thompson, John Claypool, and Jim Evans, all special ministers of God.

Charles Britt, my guide, my mentor, and my friend, a light unto my path. He was my Auburn father; I was his second son.

Wayne Flynt for his example.

Bill Muse for giving me a chance. I hope I didn't let him down.

Jack Nicklaus for his combination of character, competitive spirit, class, and dignity, qualities we don't see much in one athlete anymore. Maybe in Jordan Spieth. I hope so.

The symbolism of John Wayne and the Lone Ranger, hero of my youth.

Ed Lee Spencer, for his example.

Neil Davis, the bravest, most courageous and principled newspaper editor I've ever known, and Jerry Elijah Brown, who taught me by example that boys from small towns could make it at Auburn.

Coach Bryant.

C.M. Newton, who taught me that you didn't have to dislike a man just because he worked at Alabama.

Charley Thornton, who, even though I went to Auburn, took me under his wing and taught me all he knew. I am honored and blessed to be one of Charley's boys.

Dave Cawood of the NCAA, my best friend and the best athletics administrator I've ever known; Roger Valdiserri, Notre Dame; Don "the Fat Fox" Bryant, Nebraska; Paul Manasseh, LSU; and Donn Bernstein, ABC, everybody's best and loudest friend; and Mark Carlson, CBS. Bo Jackson was a great football player, but without the help, advice, and input of these men, he would not have won the Heisman Trophy.

Elmore "Scoop" Hudgins of the SEC; Steve Townsend of LSU, the SEC, and later Alabama, a very dear friend with whom, sadly, I have lost contact. Andy Rogers and Mickey Holmes of the Sugar Bowl; Marvin West of the *Knoxville News-Sentinel.*

Roy Exum of the *Chattanooga News-Free Press,* who

appreciated the humanity of the people he wrote about more than any sportswriter I've ever known or read; John Pruett, Auburn and Huntsville, among reporters and editors, the fairest of the fair.

Claude Felton, Georgia, UGA, my soul brother, brought together in 1981 in the days and hours when it appeared that Vince Dooley, another man who has influenced my life, would come to Auburn.

And Pat Dye, who taught me how to compete effectively and without malice. Our opponents make us better.

Jerry McIntosh, "Pops," who trusted me enough to let me marry his beloved daughter, and Jim Mathews, my doctor and my friend. If only I had listened to him more.

The purpose of this piece is not so much to tell you about the men who have influenced my life as it is to encourage you to think about the men who have made a difference in your life and to suggest and encourage, even urge, you to reach out and tell them they mattered. And continue to matter.

Yes, it all starts with our fathers—our daddies—but there are many more men to think about and to be grateful for as this Father's Day approaches.

So many more.

Where would we be, who would we be, without their influence in our lives?

Fourth of July

It's a great country.

I get mad at it. I get irritated by it. I disagree with it and sometimes get downright angry with it.

But it's still a great country.

I sometimes don't agree with the president, and I'm sick and tired of Congress. Send 'em home. Send 'em all home. No matter the party, send 'em all home.

But it's still a great country.

It has done more to alleviate human suffering and to stand up for the rights and dignity of man (men and women) than any country in the history of the world.

It is not a perfect country, but it is a great country,

I especially get irritated with its supposed leaders. O, how I get irritated—"mad" is a better word—at its so-called leaders. Sometimes they are so childish and selfish that they won't even speak to one another, much less work together as they should.

But it is still a great country.

Yes, there are problems and concerns, challenges and

controversies. There are plenty of reasons to be mad and plenty of reasons to be angry and frustrated.

But it's still a great country.

Perhaps we are at fault, looking for, and expecting, perfection in the country and its leaders.

Perhaps we would do well to think back to our forefathers, the founders of our country, not as we make them out to be, all wise and all knowing, but as they really were.

They were not perfect people as we sometimes think them to be or want them to be. They were men (and women) just like us. They had their hopes and dreams. They had their fears and frustrations as we have our fears and frustrations. They had their moments of anger too. They had their uncertainties and questions.

Will this this thing we are trying to establish, this new country, will it work? Will it stand? Can it survive? There are so many questions, so many challenges, and so many unknowns. Will it ever work? Can it work?

They had their questions and concerns. They had their hopes and fears, but they formed a great country.

When they got mad, argued with one another, and couldn't agree on the wording of the Declaration of Independence or the Constitution, at the end of the day, they left what is now known as Independence Hall and walked to City Tavern a few blocks away.

There, while enjoying a few tankards of ale, rum, or

another beverage of choice, they talked through issues that had divided and angered them during the day. They reached agreement and formally approved those compromises and agreements the next day at Independence Hall. That's how the country was founded, how it came to be. We need more of that today.

They formed the beginnings of a great nation. Yet, they were not all wise, all knowing, or particularly visionary as we think them to be. They were men, just like you, just like me. Imperfect people doing the best they could in an imperfect world. Like you, like me.

For all their imperfections and disagreements, they formed a great country. Not a perfect country, mind you, but a great country, one that has adapted and changed over the years but a great country still, the greatest and grandest on earth.

Even when we are mad and frustrated about this or that, it is still a great country. I take great comfort in the words of George W. Bush—yes, George *W.* Bush.

He said the country, our nation, "is like a great ship upon the sea. Sometimes it veers right, sometimes it veers left, but it keeps moving forward, always finding an even keel."

I like that; I find comfort in that.

Stephen Decatur, a hero of our fledgling navy in the war against the Tripoli pirates in 1804, said something we need to think about today: "May she always be right, but my country right or wrong."

Or, as we might say today, "My country right or wrong, still my country."

John Adams said it best in a letter to his beloved Abigail on July 3, 1776, the day before independence was officially and formally proclaimed. This day, he said, "ought to be celebrated by pomp and parade, with shows, games, sports, guns, bells, bonfires and illuminations from one end of the continent to the other."

So let us do as ole John Adams said do. We have every reason to.

Because even when we are mad or irritated, as we often are, it is still a great country. And it is our home.

Cause for celebration on this and every Fourth of July.

For as long as Old Glory paints the breeze.

My New York

Start spreading the news…

Those four words from "New York, New York," Frank Sinatra's ode to the greatest city on earth, the "city that never sleeps," stir my soul.

I can't hear that song, those four words in particular, "Start spreading the news," without wanting to go there, to be there. No city on earth has more energy and excitement than New York, the Big Apple. It energizes me to go, to even think about going.

My love for New York is well known, and people often ask about the best way to enjoy a trip to the city, especially for first timers, rookies. Here is some of the advice they receive, high spots only.

Embrace the city.

Enjoy and experience everything it has to offer. There's no need to be afraid. Respectful, yes, but no more respectful or afraid than in Atlanta or any other big city. That's the most important advice anyone could give: to enjoy New York, embrace it. Embrace the city, and the city will embrace you.

Enjoy the people of New York. Yes, they talk a little funny sometimes, but that's part of the fun. They, most likely, enjoy hearing us talk as much as we enjoy hearing them talk. It all works out.

New Yorkers by and large are friendly people. Maybe not as outgoing in the same way we southerners are but friendly nonetheless. The real concern is not the New Yorkers but the tourists, many of whom are loud, brash, pushy, and rude. New Yorkers have to tolerate them, too, as we do. Don't judge New York by the tourists; just don't be a tourist yourself.

As for specific thoughts:

Where to stay: Times Square is in the heart of everything, especially the Theatre District. The Marriott Marquis is exceptional. It has 1,400 rooms or more, enough for every person in the small town where I grew up to have their own private room with a couple hundred or so left over. The service, warmth, and hospitality are exceptional. From the moment you arrive, the Marquis makes you feel wanted and welcome, at home.

What to do: Spend time in Times Square, Crossroads of the World. There is no better place on earth for people-watching. Eat lunch from a street vendor. The food is quite good.

Ride the subway. This is a not-to-be-missed traditional New York experience. Just know where to get off and where not to get off. There are maps in each car, but know where you want to get off before you board. The maps are best used to indicate how far you are from your stop.

Ride in the yellow cabs. That, too, is a not-to-be-missed New York experience. The faster the cabbies drive, the more desperately and erratically they honk their horns, the more memorable the experience.

For a nicer, slower but less exciting ride, and to guarantee your ride will be where you want it when you want it, try Uber. Impressive rides with impressive drivers. It may cost a little more but is well worth it if you want guaranteed efficiency and not uncertainty and excitement.

First-time visitors to New York should take the Circle Line Cruise to understand that Manhattan really is an island and to get a good feel of the city, what's where, that kind of thing.

A trip on the Staten Island ferry should be on any New York to-do list. The ferry travels from the tip of Manhattan to Staten Island and back, departing every thirty minutes. It is a can't-miss experience, especially when ridden at night.

The skyscrapers of Lower Manhattan seem to magically rise as you sail to Staten Island. The colors and transformation of the city are amazing. The ferry, a free ride, offers close-up views of the Statue of Liberty and Ellis Island. You might want to ride it more than once. It is free, and there's not much free in NYC.

The Statue of Liberty. I sometimes wonder how much longer Emma Lazarus's immortal words, "Give me your tired, your poor, your huddled masses yearning to breathe free ... I lift my lamp beside the golden door," will be etched on the pedestal where Lady Liberty stands. It seems as if we, as a nation, are trying to erase those words and their promise more and more with every passing day. That, too, is another rant for another day.

The absence of the Twin Towers of the World Trade Center has a sad, sobering effect, but Freedom Tower will make you proud. The 9-11 Museum at Ground Zero tells a tragic, tragic story, but in the end, there is inspiration too. All those NYPD and NYFD police and firemen, continuing to go up when the whole world seemed to be coming down. These United States of America can be knocked down, but we will always rise again. Always.

Observation decks at the Empire State Building and the relatively new Top of the Rock at Rockefeller Center offer expansive and impressive views of the vastness of the city and its many towering skyscrapers.

Go to Grand Central Station early enough in the afternoon to watch the rush hour develop. Watch it come and watch it go. View it from the second floor to fully appreciate how, in the right situation, we humans become like ants, rushing to and fro. Grand Central is the transportation hub, not just of New York but of the entire northeast. It is a busy place.

Spend some time in Central Park. Enjoy the ambiance and, again, the many variations of people you will see. Take a carriage ride if you like, but be sure to spend most of your park time in Bryant Park located behind the New York Public Library not too far from the Marquis.

Join New Yorkers for lunch hour at Bryant Park. Get some vendor food; remember, it is quite good. Find a place to sit, relax, and watch thousands of workers leave the cramped, narrow confines of their offices for a few minutes of fresh air and sunshine. On a clear day, Bryant Park, with its massive green trees moving gently against an Auburn-blue sky, is the most peaceful, soothing, and relaxing place in the city. New York has done a good job of protecting its parks and providing open green space for its people.

Where to eat? Have dinner at Carmine's on Forty-Fourth Street. Large, very large, portions of Italian food served family style. For seafood, the Oyster Bar at Grand Central is good. Forget Sardi's. The food is overpriced, and the ambience is not as good as advertised. Not worth the price. Have a sandwich at Carnegie Deli, a traditional New York deli on Seventh Avenue. Walk in hungry; you won't leave hungry.

New York offers a plethora of good steak places, "steak houses," as they are called in the city. Gallagher's, 228 West Fifty-Second Street, is a traditional but somewhat unique steak house, as is Smith & Wollensky's on Forty-Ninth Street at Third Avenue. Reservations are recommended at both.

For historical interest, try Sparks on East Forty-Sixth Street. Paul (Big Paul) Castellano, described by the *New York*

Daily News as "the kingpin of American organized crime," was gunned down in the street after enjoying what proved to be his last meal. He died a well-fed man. That much is certain. He was killed on December 17, 1985, just a few days after Bo Jackson received his Heisman Trophy. No correlation, of course, just an interesting frame of reference.

For years, waiters and staff at Sparks refused to talk about Castellano's murder, but now they talk about it freely. Someone, perhaps the guy(s) who planned the hit or carried it out, must have died.

Go see the Yankees play. Stay until the last out is made, and win or lose, hear "Ole Blue Eyes," Frank Sinatra, sing "New York, New York" as no one else can do. "Start spreading the news ... I'm leaving today." It is a great New York moment. I smile thinking about it.

Go to a Broadway show. *The Phantom of the Opera*, the longest-running show in Broadway history, will move your heart, but *Les Misérables* could change your life. It is about mercy, those who give it and those who cannot understand or accept it. Therein lies life's greatest tragedy. It's Val Jean and Javert, two of the greatest names in literary history and now theatrical history.

Buy your theatre tickets online with Ticketmaster or Telecharge. You can pick your own seats that way and avoid the 30–50 percent markup hotel brokers charge. TKTS is a half-price ticket agency in Times Square, but the supply is often limited and is virtually nonexistent for the most popular shows. If you are going to see a show on Broadway in New York, get a good ticket and see a good show. You owe it to yourself.

Don't miss the Rockettes at Radio City Music Hall. Those ladies, some of whom are much more chronologically gifted than you might imagine, can kick and dance in ways you can't imagine. They are quintessentially New York.

Should you be in New York during the holidays, don't miss Radio City Music Hall's Christmas Spectacular, perhaps the best holiday show ever staged. Walk across the street to Rockefeller Center and see ice-skaters and the Christmas tree. Seeing them in person is special.

Try some of those "chestnuts roasting on an open fire," that Nat King Cole sings about so beautifully. Their aroma is irresistible, their taste something less, but they are worth trying just because it's Christmas, Christmas in New York.

Take a walk down Fifth Avenue any day of the year but especially during Christmas.

If you are going up for Auburn's basketball game against Boston College at Madison Square Garden on December 12, you should, by all means, use the travel package the Athletics Department or the Alumni Association is certain to offer. The Christmas holidays, between Thanksgiving and New Year's, are the most expensive time of the year to be in the city, and travel agencies will have already negotiated the best possible rates.

And if, by chance, if you are in New York on a Saturday in the fall, go to the Green Market at Union Square in Greenwich Village. Farmers from Connecticut and New Jersey bring their farm-raised produce into the city and sell directly to the people—a farmer's market in the heart of New York City. When you see bunches of autumn leaves for sale, you know you are not in the South anymore.

Not that you needed to be reminded anyway.

It's a long way from the Backbooth at Chappy's to New York City, but a part of my heart, a part of my soul, makes that journey every day.

Too Much Football

I love football. But there is such a thing as too much football. Twenty-four hours a day, seven days a week, fifty-two weeks a year, football, football, football. Football infinitum. Football ad nausea.

All winter long, all spring long, all summer long, football, football, football. By the time we actually get to football season, as we are now, we are already worn out.

All too many players getting in trouble, here, there, everywhere. This coach is going here, this coach going there, who's mad at whom, and whose feelings are hurt because of some perceived slight, real or otherwise.

And all the coach-speak. It seems as if no one, no coach at least, has ever had an original thought, much less knows how to express it.

Jabber, jabber, jabber. It's like that ole poem we had to learn as kids, "Jabberwocky," I believe it was. Jabber, jabber, jabber, jabberwocky.

And the internet has made it even worse, not at all good for the game. Rumor here, rumor there, rumor everywhere.

And somebody, many somebodies actually, are stupid enough or naïve enough to believe it. "Well, I read on the internet," they say. Give us a break! Give all of us a break! Give college football a break!

Just because you read it on the internet doesn't make it true. It has a better than even chance of not being true.

And we used to think talk shows were bad!

And recruiting! It's the worst of all, totally ridiculous, totally out of hand.

This seventeen-year-old is going to Auburn today, to Alabama tomorrow, and to Florida, Georgia, or LSU by the end of the week. It's like a teenager trying to decide who to go out with Saturday night.

It's ridiculous the amount of coverage these commitments, semicommitments, and "leaning toward" stories receive. Nobody knows for sure until signing day where these young men will go. They don't know, not really. So why worry? They are kids. Remember when you were seventeen years old? They are no different.

Where's it going to stop? Alabama offers a tenth grader, so Auburn offers a ninth grader, LSU offers an eighth grader, and Tennessee a seventh grader? It's ridiculous, bordering on stupid, for a fan base to get so wrought up.

Pretty soon we will be reading about recruiting infants. If he burps, he's going to Auburn; if he lets one fly, he's going to Alabama. Feel free to change that to favor your school.

Next thing you know, Gus Malzahn will be in the waiting room only to find that Nick Saban is in the delivery room, both with scholarships in hand. It's crazy; it's ridiculous.

But ole Pat Dye has already done them one better. In the early eighties, he had a great defensive tackle, Doug Smith, who was dating an equally great women's basketball player, Becky Jackson. Both were athletic specimens coaches dream about.

Dye took great delight in telling alumni and friends that he had already told Doug and Becky that if they got married and had any children, "chilluns" as he called them, he guaranteed them a scholarship to Auburn, especially if they had a "boy baby." They never did.

All of this craziness, this media jabberwocky about recruiting, is reminiscent of a book that was once written about Texas football. It was titled *Meat on the Hoof*, all too often an appropriate name for football recruiting in colleges and high schools.

But we all know high schools don't recruit. Right? Yeah, right.

I am reminded of a situation that happened long ago, back in the eighties, in the Dye era.

There was a player in the Birmingham area who was the best, the absolute best, maybe the best football player God ever created. He was Tracy Rocker, Cam Newton, Pat Sullivan, Bo Jackson, Aundray Bruce, and Nick Fairley all rolled into one.

Throw in Lee Roy Jordan, John Hannah, Cornelius Bennett, Joe Namath, Ken Stabler, and Mark Ingram too. This kid, whose name I have long since forgotten, was that good. Or was supposed to be.

Naturally, the *Birmingham News* rated him the No. 1 player in the state. But he committed to Auburn, and the next week the *News* rated him the fourth or fifth best player in the state. Go figure.

That's a true story, the moral of which is, don't pay attention—at least not too much attention—to those four-, five-, six-, seven-, or eight-star ratings any more than you would a campaign speech by Hillary or The Donald.

"What matters is not so much who you get but what you do with the ones you do get," Coach Dye said, and he was right, as right as right can be.

"When you sign all those four or five stars," he added, "sometimes you have to 'un-recruit' them to get them to buy into the team concept."

Now, at last, we are getting to when it matters. As John Wayne said in *The Undefeated*, "The talk's dried up." The real football season starts now.

I am reminded of a line George C. Scott had in the movie *Patton*, "War. God help me, I do love it so." That's the way I feel about football. I do love it so.

Every Saturday is like those Greek city-state wars we read about in high school or college ancient history classes.

Both sides come to the battlefield, in our case a hundred-yard battlefield, banners flying, drums beating, soldiers and camp followers shouting, cheering, yelling, and hollering, sometimes in unison, sometimes not, all ready to do battle to see who is best. It's college football in the twenty-first century.

As this football season approaches, as grand and glorious as it may be and as much as we love it, we would be wise to consider what we read and hear. What appears to be true, what the public and media rush to believe is true, may not be true at all. Perhaps even the figment of someone's fertile imagination.

That said, let the games begin. The time has come. The Ws and Ls will do the talking from now on. That's the only talk that really matters

As for me and my house, we say, "War Eagle!"

And mean it.

Compromise

Every politician has to compromise. The problem comes when they compromise themselves beyond recognition.

In Sickness and in Health ...

The group Alabama has a song, "Angels Among Us." The chorus goes something like this: "I believe there are angels among us, sent down to us from somewhere up above. They come to you and me in our darkest hours to show us how to live, to teach us how to give. To guide us with the light of love ..."

I write of such an angel today.

We all know that behind every great man, there is a great woman. Fran Davidson is the great woman behind Buddy Davidson, BD or Buddy D as he is called. "Mr. Auburn" would be a more appropriate name, but to Fran, he is simply "my sweet BD."

We all know, most of us at least, about Buddy's streak of having seen every Auburn football game since the start of the 1957 season. It covers fifty-nine years and 681 games. It is the longest perfect attendance streak in Auburn history and one of the longest in college football history. He has never seen Auburn play on television, and in this day and age, that is quite a distinction.

But this isn't a story about Buddy D. ("Mr. Auburn"); this is a story about Fran, her love, her care, her compassion, and her goodness. She is one of those angels among us that Alabama sings about.

The wise among us know that a person can have no greater love than to lay down his or her life, his or her hopes and dreams, for another person.

That is what Fran Davidson has done for Buddy. She has lain down her life for him, enabling him to have a quality of life that would not be possible without her. Without her, he would be in a nursing facility, unable to do or participate in any of the things that give his life quality and meaning.

His life has become her life, her reason for being. She takes care of his every need. She bathes him, dresses him, chauffeurs him, and helps him be understood when he tries to speak and the words just don't come out right.

Never will you find a woman who exemplifies that part of the marriage vow "in sickness and in health" more so than Fran Davidson.

They were married in 2001, a second marriage for both. They looked forward to spending their golden years together, sharing them with family, friends, and Auburn football. Always Auburn football. They especially enjoyed riding Buddy's Harley, a two-seater that took them everywhere they wanted to go. They rode together, laughed together, and smiled together. Their love was evident to all who saw them.

Then came September 23, 2014, and their lives changed forever. A stroke left Buddy's left side paralyzed and his speech greatly impaired, almost impossible to understand, except for Fran. Their way of life, the way they were going to spend their golden years, changed in a matter of minutes. Gone. Gone forever.

There were unimaginable unanticipated challenges. They have done well, better than expected. But it's not easy, and it's especially hard on Fran. Not every person could do what she feels called to do.

Facebook (Fran Wall Davidson) has become an escape of sorts for Fran. Her posts are a microcosm of life for all of us.

She is irritated when deer eat her flowers in the spring but moved almost beyond words when those same deer give birth to fawns in her backyard. She shares her love for beauty and nature, which is all around us if only we have eyes to see. Fran has such eyes, eyes that love and appreciate.

Her Facebook posts record her frustration and indignation at times. Recently, several grown, healthy-looking men sat and watched as she struggled to get Buddy's wheelchair through a series of doors at the doctor's office. "They could have at least offered to help," she wrote. "What happened to courtesy and thoughtfulness?"

Most of her posts are about her "Sweet BD." She writes

about their love for each other and poignantly about the changes time and circumstance have brought to their lives.

"Happy Anniversary to the love of my life. You are my sunshine, my only sunshine; you make me happy when skies are gray. You'll never know, dear, how much I love you, please don't take my sunshine away …"

"My sweet BD is and will be my last true love 'til death do us part. Our love for each other never stops growing …"

She writes about small accomplishments of their lives, like moving from a one-hand walker to a cane.

She encourages friends to talk to him even though they can't understand his words. She is there to interpret, and it is important to him that he still be part of the conversation.

She writes of his love of football, all of college football, not just Auburn football.

When they married, her Sweet BD had three televisions and three remotes in their den, a remote control for each TV. That way, he said, he could keep up with every game worth watching. Now they are down to one TV and one remote. One of the ways in which time has taken its toll.

"We sold our Harley over the holidays," she once wrote. "So sad to see it go … so much fun and so many good memories.

"Our Sweet BD stood in the driveway and watched it go until it was out of sight …"

But this is not meant to be a sad story, a pity party of sorts. It is meant to be just the opposite, a beautiful story of love. It is the story of a good woman who loves her husband and is intent on seeing him enjoy life, their life, no matter the challenges and no matter the costs to her. Hers is a sacrificial love.

They have chosen not to mourn what is past but to celebrate what is.

Thus, come Saturday, she will help him shower and shave. They will have lunch, and she will dress him in his finest Auburn colors.

And when his beloved Auburn Tigers take the field to play Clemson, he will be right where he should be, in his seat next to the press box, ready to start his sixtieth season of Auburn football by watching his Tigers play for the 682nd straight game.

Angels among us?

Sure, I'm blessed to know one.

And Buddy Davidson, "Mr. Auburn," is blessed to be married to one.

Buddy and Fran

Offensive Woes

Auburn's offensive woes remind me of a story from long ago, fifty years ago in fact, 1966.

Unfortunately offensive woes are not uncommon in Auburn football, and that year, the offense was especially woeful.

One fan had finally had enough. "Fire Bradberry!" he shouted again and again from his seats in section 6, Auburn's premier seating section. He was referring to Buck Bradberry, Auburn's offensive coach and quarterback coach, in the days before designations such as offensive coordinator and defensive coordinator became in vogue.

"Fire Bradberry! Fire Bradberry! Fire Bradberry!" he shouted over and over, again and again. "Fire Bradberry!"

Finally, the man sitting in front of him had enough. Turning around, he said, "Hell, man. Bradberry's not even on the staff anymore. He's been at the alumni association for two years."

"Oh!" the man said, startled. Then he began to shout, "Bring back Bradberry, bring back Bradberry, bring back Bradberry …"

Such is life.

Especially for a football coach.

Forgive and Forget?

Forgive and forget.
 We should do that because it's in the Bible, right?
Wrong.
"Forgive and forget" is not in the Bible. Not even once.
You might be surprised at what's not in the Bible if you took time to read it.
Forgive and forget is from Shakespeare, in four different plays written over a twenty-year period.
He must have been fond of those words, that phrasing, and the concept that went with them. "Forgive and forget." One could wonder what was going on in his life that those words should seem so important. Was he reinforcing a need from within? Or was he simply reminding his audiences of what he considered to be an eternal truth?
Forgive and forget?
No.
We aren't made to forget.
But we are made to forgive.
Forgiving means letting go, moving on, not letting what

happened in the past hold sway over our future. It does not mean forgetting.

We can't forget. God didn't make us that way. We are made to forgive, and in forgiving, we no longer allow the hurts, slights, grudges, and anger of the past, the scars and bruises of the past, to cripple our relationships with others.

Forgiveness is not easy. It is hard, tough, and sometimes seems impossible. On occasion, it may take some time, but forgiveness is the only way to go, the only way to live a full, free, and unburdened life. In forgiving others, we free ourselves from the pain of the past.

Shakespeare had it wrong. We can't forget.

But Jesus had it right. He didn't say we had to like everybody; he said we should forgive everybody.

Forgive and move on, not forgetting but no longer held captive by shackles of the past.

Forgive.

It may be the most important thing you ever do.

The Handshake

As the university gets ready to commemorate "Fifty Years of Integration at Auburn," it is a story worth retelling. And one worth remembering.

It was January 1964, and Auburn was preparing for the admission of its first African American student, Harold Franklin, who would be enrolling in graduate school.

It was only a few months since Governor George Wallace's "Stand in the School House Door" at the University of Alabama and only a little over a year since murder, riots, and mayhem at Ole Miss. US Marshals and later federal troops had to be called in to restore order on the campus and ensure the admission of James Meredith as the first black student at Ole Miss.

Now it was Auburn's turn to do the right thing, to right a wrong that had been the norm for 108 years, since the university's founding in 1856. Auburn wanted none of what happened at Tuscaloosa and at Oxford. None.

The campus was cordoned off. Only students, faculty, and staff with ID cards were admitted, and the longed-for or loathed admission took place without incident.

Franklin had been assigned a room in one of the university's men's residence halls, Magnolia Hall, "Mag Dorm" as it was commonly called. In an effort to ensure his safety and to prevent potential confrontations with other male students, he had been given an entire floor all to himself.

But old habits, old norms, and old mores die hard.

An unofficial shunning of Franklin was taking place. Out of fear and ignorance, many if not most students refused to speak to him or to acknowledge his presence, seemingly even his humanity.

Bill Van Dyke, a starting guard on the football team, was not one of those students.

Seeing Franklin walking across campus, almost always alone, Van Dyke listened to his heart and did the right thing: he sought Franklin out, and when he found him, he extended his hand and said, "Hi. I'm Bill Van Dyke. Welcome to Auburn …" It seemed a perfectly natural, normal act, he would say years later. "He was a man just like I was, and we were both trying to get an education. We were in the same boat. Why not speak to him?"

A simple act by a good man, one of the first to make an effort to help Auburn's first African American student feel welcome and at home.

Years later, Franklin doesn't remember the encounter or the handshake. Van Dyke could never forget it.

Drew Pearson, a noted nationally syndicated columnist,

heard about Van Dyke's action and mentioned it, noted it actually, in his column that appeared in major newspapers across the country.

Van Dyke immediately began to feel some degree of shunning himself, and a few death threats were not uncommon.

It bothered Van Dyke in some ways, and in other ways, the most important ways, it didn't bother him at all. "I'd done the right thing," he said, "and that's all that really matters …"

Doing the right thing. That's all that mattered then. It's all that matters now.

Because Bill Van Dyke, a football player, had done the right thing, it made it easier and more acceptable for others, those whose hearts were in the right place, to do the same.

It might not be that way now—the world has changed a lot since 1964—but that was the way it was then. Football players carried a lot of weight and influence.

Almost fifty years later, if you ask Bill Van Dyke, now an ice carver in Atlanta, what his greatest moment at Auburn was, what he remembers and cherishes most, what he is proudest of, his answer would be simply this:

"Shaking Harold Franklin's hand and trying to make him feel welcome …"

A Matter of Perspective

Question:

Why is it that when we think about others and their shortcomings, we rush to the Old Testament, a book of rules, laws, crime, and punishment, to think about how they will have to answer for what we perceive as *their* sins and transgressions, their shortcomings?

Yet, when it comes to ourselves and those we love, we rush to the New Testament, a book of love, mercy, and grace?

Could it be that we want penalty and punishment for others and love, mercy, and grace for ourselves and those we love?

That doesn't seem to be in line with what Jesus said to do, "Love thy neighbor as thyself ... Do unto others as you would have them do unto you ... Judge others as you would have them judge you ..." or something to that effect ...

So, what will it be? Old Testament punishment or New Testament grace? The choice is up to us. And how we decide may well determine what kind of Christians we are. One who talks the talk or one who walks the walk.

As we judge others, so shall we be judged ...

Something to think about ...

Lord, Gawd, Dave

"Lord, Gawd, Dave …"

That was the term my dear departed mother—who becomes more saintly as the years go by—would use when something amazing, unbelievable, improbable, and just plain stupendous happened … "Lord, Gawd …" Kind of like Mel Allen's "How-w-w A-bout That!!!" to Yankees and Alabama fans.

Momma's words came immediately to mind two weeks ago when "The Miracle at Jordan-Hare" as Rod Bramblett called it, took place. "Lord, Gawd, Dave, what happened?" Now, fourteen days later, we all know what happened, and it is still just as amazing, unbelievable, improbable and just plain stupendous as it was that night.

All of which brings to mind a question: "What would it be like if something like that happened in an Auburn-Alabama game?"

Could either side, Auburn or Alabama, stand it? Could the stadium stand it? Could the state stand it?

The answer is, of course, "yes." Fans of both sides could stand it—they would have no choice—the stadium could stand it and the state could stand it. It only seems as if the fate of the Western World, as we know it, hangs in balance with the outcome of the Auburn-Alabama game, sometimes with the outcome of every play. But life does go on. There is a tomorrow no matter how we may feel at a given time. As is written since the days of the early Persian poets, "This, too, shall pass …" And pass it does.

Both sides have had their moments of glory and heartache in this rivalry. Need I mention 17–16, 17–15, 25–23 and 28–27? There are more as well. On both sides, glory and heartache. We've seen and experienced it all, and, most likely we will see and experience it all again. Of that you can be certain. That is the nature of football and the passage of time.

But to steal victory from the clutches of certain defeat and to it with shock and awe … that is something special, something special indeed. In 60-plus years of following Auburn Football, three such games come immediately to mind: 17–16, of course, the two blocked punts; the 30–26 win over LSU in 1994, the game in which three straight LSU passes were intercepted and all were returned for touchdowns, the last coming in the very latter stages of the game, and the 1989 Florida game when Reggie Slack found Shayne Wasden streaking down the east sideline on Auburn's last play of the game to turn what appeared to be a certain 7–3 loss into a 10–7 victory.

From an Auburn standpoint those may come as close as anything could to what we—and the college football world—saw and experienced here two weeks ago.

While not as versed in Alabama football history—and that should come as no surprise to anyone—one game comes to mind, a game from long ago, Alabama's 16–15 win over Georgia Tech in Grant Field in 1960. Alabama trailed the entire game, Georgia Tech dominated. Alabama appeared to be outmanned and outclassed, beaten, but it was not to be.

This is how Benny Marshall, Sports Editor of *The Birmingham News* described it the next day: *The score was 16–15. Numbers in lights on a scoreboard. Flip a switch and they are gone, but Alabama's Crimson Tide put them there Saturday at Grant Field and left them flaming for history ... For 59 minutes, 59 seconds this was Georgia Tech's football game. Then all of a sudden, all of it was gone ..."* Alabama won the game when Richard O'Dell, who had never kicked a field goal, made a 24-yarder as time ran out. It would be the only field goal he ever kicked. *"Flip a switch and they are gone ..."* but those numbers and that game are still remembered, even by an Auburn man, 53 years later.

And so it will be with "The Miracle at Jordan-Hare."

One can only wonder how Marshall, the dean of Southern sportswriters—then and now—would have described what happened here at Jordan-Hare two weeks ago had he lived to see and experience it.

That is what set Benny Marshall's writing apart. He not only observed an event; he experienced it and, in rare degree, he had the ability to convey the emotion of that moment to his readers. What took place against Georgia was Benny's kind of game. He was a writer, not a sportswriter. Only he could have done it justice.

But what of this day, this time, this place, this Auburn-Alabama game? One can only hope—if that one is an Auburn fan—that what was written long ago about another team comes to fruition once again: *"They believed in themselves; their destiny they knew; and they had the "stuff" to make their dream come true..."*

If their dream—our dream—comes true tonight, as improbable as it may seem to others, this much is certain:

Momma's *"Lord, Gawd, Dave"* will be far from sufficient.

As it turned out, Momma's "Lord, Gawd" was insufficient, for both Auburn fans and Alabama fans that day. This piece appeared in *Auburn Football Illustrated*, the game program on November 30, 2013, the day Auburn's Chris Davis returned a missed Alabama field goal 109 yards for the game-winning touchdown (34–28) with one second left on the clock. 0:01

There weren't enough "Lord, Gawd, what just happened?" to go around that day on either side of the stadium, Alabama or Auburn.

Turning Seventy

Turned seventy this week, and all is well. Not perfect but well. Good.

I am a blessed and fortunate man to have been born where I was—in the United States of America—to have the family I have and the many friends who have joined me in the journey.

Some have been with me all the way; others have left along the way, faded away because of time, location, and circumstance. They have all impacted my life and made me the person I am, and the person I yet hope to be.

People often say, "I wish I could start over again." I am not one of those people. Not me. My life has been so blessed, so full, so full of meaning that I would not want to start over again. There is no way it could turn out as well a second time. Yes, I wish I was younger, and I wish I didn't hurt as much, but I would not want to do it all over again. No way.

Time has taken its toll on the body. I hurt a lot, the normal aches and pains of aging, the doctors say. All the vitals are good. No undue worries there.

Age and infirmity have caused me to have to give up some

of the things I love—golf, travel, going to the beach—but I can live a good life without them. I do live a good life, a good, full life.

I walk with a cane, and on longer walks, I need a walker. I swallow my pride and use a wheelchair on some occasions, but life is good.

When I wake up in the morning, I feel like I'm thirty-five or forty. But when I get out of bed, I feel like I'm seventy, eighty, on some mornings ninety or more.

More importantly, in the ways that matter, mentally, spiritually, and emotionally, I feel young. I try to think young. Sometimes I succeed.

The older I get, the more I appreciate the wisdom of John Jeffers, longtime minister at Auburn First Baptist Church. "We think of ourselves as physical creations with a spiritual dimension" he often said, "but in reality we are spiritual creations with a physical dimension. Our bodies are subject to the laws of physics, but our spirits are subject to the laws of God."

Our bodies are but earthly vessels that house the spirit. How true, how true. Our bodies don't define who we are; our spirits do.

I don't know how much longer I will live. None of us do. Shakespeare had it right when he had Julius Caesar say, "It seems to me most strange that men should fear death, seeing that death, a necessary end, will come when it will come." Or something like that.

I don't fear death; it's the dying I fear. Like all of us, I hope it is quick and easy. I want to die in my sleep. Few people do.

I don't want to be kept alive by machines and special means. A man can live too long. I don't want to exist; I want to live.

What will life be like beyond the veil? I have no idea, but I hope it will be more than streets of gold and walls of jasper. The earthly trappings of wealth and power have no place in heaven, whatever and wherever that may be.

I believe there will be people of many faiths in the hereafter, people who have earnestly sought to know God in the best way they knew how. As Christians, we believe that God is a God of love, that God that seeks us, and that he responds to those who seek him. I do not believe that he seeks only us. I do not believe he responds to us alone.

I am not prepared to limit God. I am not prepared to say that God must speak to all of his children in the same way he speaks to me. If I say that, I am limiting the power of God, and I refuse to do that. It's up to God who gets in and who doesn't, and I leave that up to him. He will make the right choices; of that I am certain.

I believe in the resurrection and immortality of the spirit, not the body. My theologian friends tell me that is Greek thought, not Christian thought, but so be it. That's the way God has spoken to me.

There will be a resurrection of the spirit but not a

resuscitation of our earthly bodies. I've never been a big fan of Paul, but I believe he is right when he says we will have resurrection bodies—a spiritual resurrection in a spiritual body, not a human body. I will be with Jesus. Nothing else matters.

Approaching seventy has caused me to appreciate more and more the line from "My Way" that Frank Sinatra sings so well: "Regrets I've had a few, but then again, too few to mention …"

I've had my share of regrets, "but then again, too few to mention." All we can do, all we are asked to do, is to make the best decisions we can make at the time we have to make them. Then move on, unencumbered by the past.

If I have hurt anyone, angered anyone, or slighted anyone, I apologize, and I hope you will grant an old man the forgiveness he seeks.

As my friend and mentor in all things spiritual, Charles Britt, used to say, "Our whole lives will be spent trying to bridge the gap between where we are and where we ought to be, from who we are to who we ought to be."

Seventy years in, and I'm still on that journey. With God's help and your love, patience, and understanding, I will have closed that gap a little more tomorrow than I have today.

I hope I have made a difference along the way, a difference for good, especially in the lives of young people. Having that opportunity is one of the great blessings of living in a college town. Opportunity awaits every day. Aches, pains, and all, there is still work to do in the vineyard.

The road ahead still beckons.

Even at seventy, the best is yet to come.

Voices

The voices of negativity are always louder than the voices of progress.

The Bear Facts

Did you know that bears can run up to fifty feet, or seventeen yards, in one second?

Think of that in terms of first downs in football, almost two first downs in one second. One single second: 00:01. A lot can happen in one second.

Researcher Sylvia Dolson has found that bears can run up to thirty-seven miles an hour, twice as fast as Olympic sprinters and faster than race horses over short distances. They are not so much running as they are bounding, but as one of God's greatest creations, bears can move, really move.

Black bears are gradually making a comeback in Alabama, a place where they once roamed freely as the dominant animal species in the land.

There are at least 164 known bears living permanently in Alabama, thirty-two in and around the Talladega National Forest in northeast Alabama and 132 in extreme southwest Alabama, in and around the Tensaw River delta north of Mobile. Ongoing research indicates there may be as many as two to three hundred bears living in Alabama, but the numbers, at this point, are inconclusive.

These numbers were determined by DNA studies of bear scat and hair samples collected by Auburn University's School of Forestry and Wildlife Sciences. Bear scat is a scientific term for bear poop.

These are just the bears that live here. Many more are passing through Alabama, however, and their numbers are increasing annually.

These traveling bears, almost always young males, are coming from northwest Georgia and southwest Mississippi. Some, like those that pass through the Auburn area, occasionally come from central Georgia near Macon.

They either struck out on their own or, at about two and a half years (thirty months) old, were turned away by their mother because she was ready to mate again. In some cases, they could have been chased away by a larger bear determined to make their home his home. Whatever the case, they are coming this way.

Bears passing through Alabama are looking for three things: a mate, a plentiful food supply, and a place to call home, a range or territory of their own. Of the three, food is first, the girlfriend second. In that sense, male bears aren't that much different from their human counterparts. Food and females.

Bears occasionally seen along the highway and in rural

areas near small towns are most likely bears passing through Alabama but not establishing a range here. Not yet. Alabama is not attractive to young males at this point because there are so few females here.

Female black bears typically live within a range of about one and a half square miles, and they tend to stay close to that home territory. Male bears, even with a territory of thirteen square miles, tend to roam.

Since females are homebodies and there are so few in Alabama, it is not likely that Alabama will have a substantial bear population anytime soon, but the bears are coming back, back to a land that once belonged more to their ancestors than to ours.

Black bears, such as we have in Alabama and the South, are not inherently dangerous.

A recent study of black bear attacks in the United States, Canada, and Alaska revealed that there have been only fifty-nine fatal black bear attacks in the last 110 years. Only fifty-nine fatal black bear attacks in all of the United States, Canada, and Alaska combined in 110 years!

According to Dr. Todd Steury, bear expert and researcher extraordinaire in Auburn University's School of Forestry and Wildlife Sciences and the black bear's best friend in Alabama, there is a greater likelihood of dying from a bee attack than from a bear attack.

Bees kill about fifty-three people per year in the US. So

about as many people are killed by bees in one year as were killed by black bears in 110 years.

If, however, you should get into a confrontation with a bear, which statistics show is extremely unlikely, don't run. That would be the worst thing you can do, given the bear's aforementioned speed and quickness.

To defend yourself from what might turn into a confrontation with a bear, scare the bear away by making yourself as large, as loud, and as intimidating as possible.

Spread your arms like a windmill, wave your hands, and make as much noise as possible. Yell at the bear, throw things at the bear. If he continues to come toward you, be prepared to fight back. Hit him and kick him. Especially try to hit him in the nose and gouge his eyes. Bears don't like to have their eyes gouged or noses busted any more than humans do.

Given the chance of running or fighting, the bear will run. The bear is far more afraid of you than you are of the bear.

The one exception, of course, is a mother and her cubs. As cute and beautiful as the cubs may be—and they are cute and beautiful—don't go anywhere near them, and never, ever get between a mother bear and her babies. That's the worst thing you can do to provoke a bear—and that would be more your fault than the bear's fault. Watch and admire the cubs, yes, but do it from afar, not up close and personal.

And finally, bears in Alabama and the South do not hibernate as they do in other parts of the country. Bears here go into what is called a state of torpor in which they take long naps that can vary in length from two or three days to ten days or more, depending on the bear. They wake up, eat a bit, and then go back to their nap.

Bears don't hibernate because of cold weather but because of reduced food supply. In warmer climates such as Alabama and most of the South, there is ample vegetation for food supply the year around. Bears don't eat people; they eat fruits, nuts, berries, seed pods, and fungi.

If you are fortunate enough to have a bear in your backyard or near your home, be aware of him, but there is no rational need to fear him. Respect him, but don't fear him.

The worst thing you can do—other than kill him, which is against the law and carries severe penalties—is to feed a bear. Dr. Steury says, "A fed bear is a dead bear." Feeding a bear causes it to become increasingly dependent on human-supplied food sources rather than on its natural ability to find and secure food for itself. There is no such thing as a pet bear.

Campus lectures are one of the best things about living in a college town. Most of the material you have just read comes from a recent lecture by Dr. Steury on the black bear's return to Alabama.

To learn more about the bears that are slowly but steadily and surely coming our way, contact the Alabama Black Bear Alliance in Millbrook (1-800-822-9453 or Awf@alabamawildlife.org). In cooperation with the Alabama

Wildlife Federation, the Black Bear Alliance's goal, objective, and purpose is to "Restore, Protect and Conserve" the black bears as they make their return to Alabama.

I love bears. And I believe, given the chance, you will learn to appreciate them too. They are fascinating animals, one of God's greatest creations, and they are about to become our neighbors again.

Respect them, but there is no need to fear them.

Frustrated Jesus

A frustrated Jesus in Roland Merullo's wonderful book *American Savior: A Novel of Divine Politics*: "I didn't come to be worshipped. I came to be emulated."

Lot of truth in that.

If we who call ourselves Christians would spend less time worshipping him and more time living the life he said to lead, the world would be a lot better off. And so would we.

"I didn't come to be worshipped. I came to be emulated."

Don't worship; live as he said to live.

That is the only true worship.

Completing the Circle

What is sure to be my most memorable moment of the 2016 football season happened this past weekend, not at the Mississippi State game but before it.

Auburn, as we know, spent Friday night in Tuscaloosa and then drove to Starkville the morning of the game.

Highway 82, the road they traveled, runs through Gordo, the small town where I grew up and, to some extent, I still call home.

When I was a kid, many, many years ago, one of the highlights of football season was to sit by the side of the road and watch the Mississippi State football team and entourage come through on its way to play Alabama in Tuscaloosa.

Auburn didn't play Mississippi State in Starkville in those days. As a kid, I always thought if, if just for once, I could sit by the side of the road and watch my team, the Auburn Tigers, come through my hometown, that would be one of the coolest, neatest things ever.

All kinds of scenarios played out in my mind that could make that happen, but it never did. Not when I was a kid.

Sometimes I imagined what it would be like to ride on one of those busses, to ride through my hometown with the Auburn football team. Oh, how proud I would have been of my hometown and of my Auburn Tigers.

Later, of course, it came to pass. I did just that as a member of the Auburn athletics staff. It was touching, almost emotional, to ride through my hometown, to watch it speed by, having once been a part of it, having once been that little boy by the side of the road, wishing, dreaming, and now being a part of it—a part of Auburn, something bigger and better than I was or ever thought I could be, while sitting by the side of the road watching the busses go by.

That thought came to mind Saturday as the Auburn Tigers drove through my hometown once again.

Only this time I was by the side of the road again, with my wife, my brother, and my grandnephew, one too young to take it in or understand any of it really.

The others waved and cheered. I sat there silently, watching the busses glide by, having gone from that little boy sitting by the side of the road so long ago to an old man sitting by the side of the road once again, watching what was once his world go by.

I had come full circle.

It felt good. It felt complete.

It felt whole.

Listening to the Founding Fathers

We tend to put our country's founding fathers high atop a pedestal, revering them, almost worshipping them.

Perhaps we should listen more to what they say.

Consider these words from Benjamin Franklin as recorded by James Madison near the end of what had been a fractious, contentious Constitutional Convention:

> There are several parts of this constitution which I do not at present approve, but I am not sure I shall never approve them.
>
> For having lived long, I have experienced many instances of being obliged by better information or fuller consideration to change opinions even on important subjects which I once thought right, but found to be otherwise.

It is therefore that the older I grow, the more apt I am to doubt my own judgement, and to pay more respect to the judgement of others.

Good advice then; better advice now.

Was I Wrong?

After all these years, could I be wrong?

I am a Christian, a believer who has, for the most part, tried to follow the Way.

But I am also a believer, a strong believer, in separation of church and state, especially when it comes to mandatory school prayer.

Forced prayer in schools and at any public, state-sponsored event or gathering is wrong. It goes against something we, as Americans, *say* we believe and stand for: freedom of religion.

If it's our religion, it's okay, but if it's someone else's religion, we're not for that. Katy bar that door for sure!

But even if it is our religion, there are problems with required public prayer. Mandatory public prayer in schools is wrong, even if it is Cristian prayer.

Think about it, and be honest. During all those prayers recited and read while we were in elementary school, even high school, did you have a prayerful, reverent attitude, or were you thinking about something else entirely: your girlfriend, how you wished you had studied harder for that upcoming test, or the dread of football practice that afternoon?

Is that prayer?

And when we, as players or fans in the stadium, stand and listen to a prayer over the loudspeaker before football games, are we really in a reverent, prayerful mood, thanking God for this and that, or did we just want the prayer to be over so our favorite team, Auburn, Alabama, you name it, could take the field and kick some ass? ("Ass" in the Bible, King James Version, so don't get all mad or self-righteous about a little perceived profanity.)

Or, even worse, when praying at a football game, are we trying to curry favor with God, to get God on our side so he will help us go out and kick butt?

Is this really prayer? If it is, then God help us.

The breakdown in our society is not caused as much by the lack of prayer in public schools as it is by the disintegration of family and family values, values best taught at home by parents who are interested in every aspect of their children's lives. Parents who are there, in the home, but more about that at another time perhaps.

All of this I truly believed until something happened not long ago that caused me to question and rethink what I so strongly and steadfastly believed.

Out of the blue, as old folks used to say (for you youngsters out there, "out of the blue" means "unexpected and unanticipated"), came a call from John Hannah.

John Hannah was quite a few years behind me in school, so I had little or no recollection of him other than his was a name I associated with my hometown of long ago.

He called because he wanted me to know how much my mother meant to him when he was in her fifth-grade class and how much she continues to mean to him even though she has been dead for more than thirty years. Thirty years. Where have they gone?

This is John's story. Let's let him tell it:

> When I was in Mrs. Housel's class, every day when we lined up to go to the lunchroom, she would make us say David's Prayer: "Let the words of my mouth and the meditation of my heart be acceptable in thy sight, O Lord, my strength and my redeemer."

He continued:

> It would be difficult to say how many times this scripture has come to mind in addition to being a very real part of my morning prayer time. I do know this: I credit Mrs. Housel for teaching me this precious word.
>
> It has been 53 years since those nine months with your mother. This is not the only 5th grade

memory I have, but it is certainly the one that is the most real and meaningful.

When I am asked what my favorite Bible verse is, I have no problem saying Psalms 19:14, and most of the time I tell how my 5th grade teacher taught her class this verse.

Did John's call cause me to change my basic beliefs?

No, not really, but he did give me cause to think and to reexamine my core beliefs about prayer in public schools, beliefs I have strongly held for many years.

Fifty-three years ago, a fifth-grade public school teacher lit a candle in John Hannah's life, a candle that continues to burn brightly even unto this day.

I've never been prouder of my momma.

Mrs. Estelle Housel, John Hannah's fifth-grade teacher

My Hero

My Daddy was a hero.

He taught me how to fish and how to hunt.

He was a good shot, one of the best in our part of the county. His friends and admirers called him "Deadeye." He didn't fish just anywhere. He fished such places as Dead River and the Alligator Hole, exotic places to a little boy, places with allure and implied danger.

With the help of his younger brother Ralph, he seined his own minnows, caught his own crickets, and knew when those precious Catawba worms were going to be on the leaves of the trees and where to find them.

He enjoyed watching the train go by with his little boy who dreamed of being a railroad engineer. Sometimes they counted boxcars. Sometimes they watched, glad to be together in the setting sun.

He grilled a mean hamburger, and he enjoyed walking up the street to watch the local baseball team play on hot summer Sunday afternoons. He enjoyed pitching washers with his brothers in the hard dirt of his mother's front yard. There was never any doubt that he loved me and never any thought that he would leave me. In those days, it was an accepted fact, a given. In these days, it is a blessing beyond compare.

My Daddy never wrote a book and, except for World War II, never went far from home. He had to take a Dale Carnegie course to learn how to feel comfortable in crowds, and the highest office he ever held when I was at home was president of the local Lion's Club.

He received the Bronze Star in World War II. He never talked about it, but Uncle Ralph, his fishing buddy, told me he got it for leading his men to safety after being surrounded by the Germans at St. Vith in the Battle of the Bulge.

He was one of seventy-five American soldiers who worked their way through fifty miles of German-held territory to make the first contact with the Russians near the end of war. *Reader's Digest* wrote about it, but Daddy never talked about it. More than forty years later, the leader on that mission, William A. Knowlton, who later became commandant at West Point, remembered him as "a good soldier."

He was seventeen when his daddy died in 1931, and there was no choice but go to work in the family hardware store. He worked for his older brother for most of his working years, selling nails, roofing, fishing tackle, shotgun shells, appliances, and everything in between.

He fell in love with a third-grade school teacher from

York, and they got married in the preacher's parlor just before he went off to North Africa to fight the Germans.

He came home from the war, built a two-bedroom house next to his mother's house, and, along with his wife, Estelle, provided a warm, loving home to two boys for more than forty-four years.

I think about my Daddy every day, but I think about him tonight because of a letter that came today. Part of it read:

> In church Sunday, Bill Davis [who grew up in our home church and later became a prominent minister in the United Methodist Church] filled in. He was talking about people who had influenced him in childhood. Said things about several people, but he mentioned his scoutmaster, Dave Housel. Said they didn't really do a lot of religious activities in Scouts, but you only had to watch Dave Housel for a short while to see that Christ was truly a part of his life.
>
> Thought you would like to know that. Of course, I'm sure you knew it years ago …

I'll never be half the man my Daddy was, but I sure am glad to be his son.

Trump and the Animals

I've tried to give President Trump the benefit of the doubt. It's been hard on occasion, on many occasions, but I have tried to give him the benefit of the doubt whenever possible.

No more.

Now he's gone too far—far, far too far—with his changes to the Endangered Species Act, which adds money and cost—the almighty dollar—to the decision of whether or not to protect endangered species, in some cases to keep them from extinction.

I would hate to be a bear, a buffalo, or an eagle in this country right now. President Trump and his minions are taking dead aim at you.

The concept of man having "dominion over the earth" as mentioned in the Bible does not mean taking the earth for your own personal use, raping it, and jeopardizing nature and the animals that share this planet with us.

Having dominion over the earth means to care for the earth, to nurture it and keep it safe for ourselves and for those who follow us.

The earth and the life upon it are not ours to do with as we please. We are only borrowing it from our children, our great-grandchildren, and their great-grandchildren.

The safety of the earth, its fullness and its wholeness, are our greatest gifts to them. It is our legacy.

Mr. Trump and his minions have no concept of this.

This is bad; it is sad; and it is dangerous.

It is enough to make one weep in sorrow and to speak up in anger and frustration. Enough is enough.

Mr. Trump, you've gone too far.

A Dark, Dark Day

By a vote of 52–47, largely along party lines, the United States Senate voted Thursday to allow hibernating bears to be shot and killed while sleeping in their dens. Also to allow wolf pups to be killed in their dens.

Brave men, real men, these people, women included, who voted to remove protection of wildlife in national wildlife refuges. In national wildlife refuges! What have we come to?

Shooting a sleeping bear? That takes real talent and bravery to do that. Real skill too, shooting a hibernating bear. Takes a real man to kill a hibernating bear.

Machismo. Real machismo.

This is the equivalent of endorsing and supporting the great buffalo hunts of the late 1880s that virtually eradicated the buffalo, a symbol of the West, from the Great Plains.

I suppose I should say, "May God have mercy on the souls of the people who voted for this dastardly act."

But I can't.

I'm not there yet.

And it may be a long time coming …

If ever.

How I Became an Auburn Man

The story has oft been told, but it is worth repeating again in this, the week of another Auburn-Alabama game.

The year was 1956.

My daddy told me that Saturday morning not to come to the store that day and that he would not be home for lunch. He was going to a football game in Birmingham, something called an Auburn-Alabama game. Maybe he said "Alabama-Auburn" game. After all these years, I'm not sure.

I was ten years old and very much wanted to be with my daddy. I couldn't understand why I couldn't go with him. It was just a football game, and we had been to many football games in our little town.

"I don't have a ticket," he said, and I couldn't understand. You could buy tickets here, in our little town; why couldn't you do that in Birmingham? My feelings were hurt. He didn't want me to go with him. I didn't understand.

He knew it, and when an Alabama man, Ralph McCafferty,

came into the hardware store, checking to see if anyone wanted to buy two tickets to the game, Daddy scarfed them up.

He called and said, "If you still want to go, be at the store in thirty minutes." I was there.

That day at Legion Field was the most magnificent thing that I, a ten-year-old boy, had ever witnessed or experienced. The glory, the majesty, the grandeur, the color, pageantry, and excitement of all, not to mention the football game.

Auburn won 34–7, but it didn't matter. I had to ask which team was Auburn and which team was Alabama.

I wrote to both schools asking for information on their football teams.

Alabama sent a media guide and a bill for one dollar. Auburn sent a media guide and a handwritten note thanking me for being an Auburn fan. It was the note that made the difference.

Alabama got its dollar—I think—but Auburn got my heart.

It has made all the difference since.

And you can bet, in my time working in the Auburn Athletics Department, every time we received a letter from a young person asking for information on the Auburn football team, that youngster got a media guide and a personal note thanking him or her for being an Auburn fan.

Someone's kindness and thoughtfulness made a difference in my life.

If it made a difference once, it could make a difference again.

And, yes, I still have that media guide sent so long ago.

From Lewis Grizzard

AUBURN, Ala.—David Housel is from Gordo, Ala. "Know what 'gordo' means in Spanish?" he asked me. I didn't know. "It means 'fat,'" he said.

David is on another diet. Frankly he is *muy gordo*, but that is okay because there is more of him to enjoy that way.

David Housel lives and works in Auburn, and I doubt he will ever leave. God forbid it, in fact. It happens to a lot of people. Out of the hinterlands they come to the campus, and they never seem to get around to leaving.

David works in the Auburn journalism department, helps with one of the nation's best collegiate newspapers, *The Plainsman*, and dabbles in anything else that stands for War Eagle.

He lives in a fraternity house on campus. "I'm the housemother," he said. Some of the boys call him "Poppa." When he told me that, I could see the pride in his face.

Respectful Man

I came to know this man a number of years ago. We once spent eight hours on a train together and drank the trip entirely too short. He is an Auburn historian, an Auburn evangelist, filled with all the spirit and allegiance one good Auburn man can hold. In David Housel's case, that amounts to bushels.

I found my own schooling elsewhere, but this quiet place settles my mind. There is another man here I respect greatly. His name is Shug Jordan. He used to coach the football team. Interviewing him, somebody once said, is like talking to your daddy. It was.

I love Auburn's football stadium because it doesn't look plastic, and the grass grows out of the ground it covers. I love Auburn people because I have been on long football trips with them and they have always been nice to me. And I love the fact that the Lord picked the outskirts of Opelika for Auburn's campus. I can't picture it anywhere else.

Liquid Nostalgia

We sat in David Housel's apartment in the fraternity house. Pretty coeds from places like Enterprise and Dothan and maybe even Opp had come over for chicken dinner. The brothers were welcoming new pledges. Faces were cleanshaven. Shoes were shined. I remembered a favorite Auburn line: "It's the only school in the country where the faculty is more liberal than the student body."

What eventually happened was this: David brought out the good stuff from Tennessee and we mixed it with Coke for the sheer nostalgia involved. He found his old Methodist Cokesbury Hymnal and we started from the front and sang it through. We sang "Love, Mercy and Grace" and "Beulah Land" twice each.

That done, he played a record that was the Auburn band and Auburn songs: *"War Eaaaaagle, fly down the field ...!"* David, all of what must have been 300 pounds of him, got up, and danced.

He put on another record. It was a recording of the final moments of a famous Auburn football game. We listened to it 30 times.

Reliving History

The year was 1972. The annual thousands were in Legion Field. Powerful Alabama led the Tigers 16–0. You probably know the rest. Auburn kicked a field goal and blocked a punt and ran it into the end zone for a touchdown. With a minute and a half to play, Auburn blocked a second Alabama punt and scored again.

As long as there are two Auburn men to talk about it, that moment—and that score, 17–16—will live on.

"How many times could you listen to that?" I asked David Housel.

"Long as I have ears," he said.

He had one more recording. It was Bear Bryant's television show following the game.

"Good afternoon, Coach Bryant," said the announcer.

"What's good about it?" interrupted the growling Bear.

David Housel laughed and laughed at that. Auburn rarely beats Alabama in football except on his record player, where it remains undefeated.

Shortly before the dawn would have caught us, we gave in to sleep. The best Auburn man I know and an outsider he trusts, both floating on an amber current from a tall bottle, drifted calmly away and dreamed of a miracle six years gone, but never to be forgotten.

David Housel Auburn's Evangelist, March 17, 1978. Reprinted with permission of the *Atlanta Journal-Constitution*.

One Way to Happiness

Want to live a less stressful, happier life? Here's how:

"You've had so much strife but you are always happy. How do you do it?"

"I choose to," he said. "I can leave myself to rot in the past, spend my time hating people for what happened, like my father did, or I can forgive and forget."

"But it's not easy."

He smiled that Frank smile. "Oh, but my treasure, it is so much less exhausting. You only have to forgive once. To resent, you have to do it all day, every day. You have to keep remembering all the bad things."

He laughed, pretending to wipe sweat from his brow. "I would have to make a list, a very, very long list and make sure I hated the people on it the right amount. That I did a very proper job of hating too: very Teutonic!"—his voice became sober—"we always have a choice. All of us."

That comes from *The Light Between Oceans*, one of the best books I've read in the last ten years.

A wise and learned man, Ezra Taft Benson, once said, "Some of the greatest battles will be fought within the silent chambers of your own soul."

And so it is, with these characters, with all of us.

That's what good books are about: imperfect people, people like us, living in an imperfect world, doing the best we can.

Read *The Light between Oceans*. You will be moved beyond compare.

Almost beyond words.

A Word on Behalf of Nick Saban, the Great Satan

Not that Nick Saban needs anyone to say word on his behalf, especially an Auburn man, but I'm going to say it anyway. I like the guy.

I like the way he wins. I like the way his teams play, the way they represent their university, the way his players represent themselves. I like the way Nick Saban handles the media. Donald Trump needs to take some lessons from Saban.

Nick Saban is in charge. He's in control. He's rock solid. The only thing I don't like about him is where he coaches, and for purposes of this piece, I can get over that.

The fact that I am so complimentary of Nick Saban in no way lessens my credentials as Auburn Man. In no way. Quality is where you find it, and Nick Saban is quality in every respect. Not to recognize that is folly, pure folly.

These words are not meant to merely praise Saban but to share an opinion of where he stands in the history of SEC football and the effect he is having on that history.

The arc of progress is not one long, smooth line. It is filled with stops and starts, lurches and stalls that come together to move us forward.

Throughout the history of SEC football, there have been coaches and eras that propelled the sport forward, times that made everyone else have to get better to compete.

The first was General Neyland at Tennessee. Among those who followed were Bobby Dodd at Georgia Tech, Bear Bryant at Alabama, Steve Spurrier at Florida, and now Nick Saban.

All contributed in their own way to making SEC football what it is today. Each was dominant in his era, and each changed the way football was played in the SEC.

Bryant brought unparalleled defensive prowess to the SEC. Steve Spurrier brought offensive genius to the SEC, making it an offensive as well as a defensive league. And now comes Saban, dominating the conference as few, if any, have done.

As an Auburn Man, I would like very much to have included Coach Jordan and Pat Dye on the list, but I cannot in good conscience do so. Coach Jordan won only about 70 percent of his games, and Coach Dye's career was not long enough, only twelve years.

What they did for Auburn is immeasurable, but this is about more than Auburn. It is about the men, Saban included, who forced SEC football to get better. Jordan and Dye were part of that, shall we say, *process*, but they were not at the vanguard of the movements.

Saban and those before him forced the members of the SEC to get better in order to compete, and the SEC did get better. No reign, no dominance, lasts forever. Ask the Romans. Ask Notre Dame, Texas, and Nebraska. Nothing remains the same. Not forever.

Auburn has had the misfortune of competing in the same state with two of the coaches who have had lasting impacts on football in the SEC, Bryant and now Saban.

Even so, Auburn has fared better than most against Alabama in the Bryant and Saban eras. Auburn has not only thrived but at times prospered.

Perhaps one of the greatest compliments that could be paid to Coach Jordan is that he survived eighteen years in the same state as Bryant, facing him year after year after year. Auburn defeated Alabama six times in the Bryant era. Only Tennessee defeated him more (seven).

Auburn has defeated Saban, "The Great Satan" as he is called in some parts of Lee County, five times in thirteen years, more than any school in the SEC. This speaks to Saban's success against his major rivals and his dominance of the SEC as a whole.

There is a growing discussion among Alabama fans, the media, and others as to who is the better coach, Bryant or Saban.

No self-respecting Auburn man would get into an extended debate on that point, but there are numbers that would seem to favor each: Bryant's dominate 25-year tenure at Alabama and his six national championships; Saban's five national championships in thirteen years.

Four of Saban's championships came in seven years, 2011–2017. That's total domination, almost, not only of the SEC but the entire nation. As they say back home, "That ain't half-bad."

There is another number that should enter into this discussion. Bryant had virtually no scholarship limitations. He could sign players, quarterbacks in particular, just to keep Auburn and other schools from getting them. Saban has only eighty-five scholarships, and there is no doubt he uses them well.

Bryant's grandfatherly-favorite-uncle down-home folksiness, his drawl and "aw shucks" style, might make him the sentimental choice among older Alabama fans, but there can be no doubt about Saban's process and the results it brings.

It will be up to historians of future generations to make the ultimate decision as to who was better, but does such a choice have to be made? The children of Israel have Abraham and Moses; why can't Alabama have Bryant and Saban? It should be enough to be the best of one's generation, as Saban and Bryant so obviously are.

Tennessee's women's athletic director, Joan Cronan, said it best when giving the invocation at the SEC spring meeting several years ago. After thanking God for our many blessings and the food we were about to eat, Joan added, "And we thank you for our opponents because they make us better."

I find it somewhat difficult to be thankful that Nick Saban is at Alabama—that's for the Alabama fans to do—but he is forcing not only Auburn but all of the Southeastern Conference to get better, to ramp up our competitiveness.

So it is and so it will always be in athletics and in every form of human endeavor.

It serves no useful purpose for Auburn or any other fan base to be overly critical of Alabama and Nick Saban or any other team or coach that enjoys hard-earned success. This is not a game of "Death by a Thousand Cuts." It's more important than that.

We should spend our time trying to get better ourselves instead of looking for opportunities to run down our opponents.

Joan had it right. Our opponents do make us better.

But not with our words, with our deeds. Our actions.

As you have read these words, my respect and high regard for Coach Saban should be readily evident.

I suppose, in Joan Cronan's broad, philosophical way of thinking, I should be thankful that Nick Saban is at Alabama, but that is hard to do.

Damn hard.

And damn near impossible …

But I still like Nick Saban.

A lot.

I just wish he wasn't at Alabama.

Nick Saban

Worth Repeating

From Backbooth at Chappy's reader, Amy Wadsworth Register: "All you have to do (to get elected in Alabama) is to convince folks that Jesus is a capitalist who liked guns and was against abortion, and you will get elected with no question."

Heading West

In the old television series *Wagon Train*, starring Ward Bond and occasionally featuring Robert Horton, did the shows always end with the wagons headed to the left of the screen, heading west?

If so, it was an amazingly subtle yet effective image.

All the adventures of life—our triumphs, failures, hopes, dreams, expectations, fears, close calls, and dangers—were lived out in the lives of the men and women traveling on that wagon train every week. Every week, a new episode featured a new challenge for someone to overcome.

Yet, in the end, at the end of that one-hour episode, those wagons were still heading west, west toward the sunset.

And so it is with the episodes of our lives; when they are over, complete, and done with, we are still headed west.

West toward the sunset.

You think about those things as you get older, and I find something comforting in that.

Heading west, toward the sunset.

But we still have miles to go.

I Was Wrong. So Wrong.
And I Apologize.

The recent dustup about Richard Spencer, founder of a controversial group called ALTright, whatever that is, speaking at Auburn brought to mind a similar situation of long ago.

The year was 1969 at the height of the Vietnam War as student protests were beginning to spread across the nation. A student organization here at Auburn invited William Sloane Coffin, chaplain at Yale University and an outspoken peace activist, to speak on campus. As innocuous as it may seem now, it was quite a controversial invitation then.

As a way of protesting the war, Coffin had urged Yale students to burn their draft cards, a clear act of civil disobedience and a violation of the law.

And now this man was coming to Auburn. Would he advocate burning draft cards here? Would students burn their draft cards here? Would this man, perceived by many as a threat to all they held dear, speak against what many considered their patriotic duty, to support our president, our country, and the war?

That his trip was being financed by university funds—student activity fees—made it dicier. This was, after all, Auburn, a conservative bastion, and it was the sixties.

The use of state funds became an issue, in reality an effort to find a way to keep Coffin from coming to Auburn. As with everything else at Auburn, then and now, the faculty got involved, the board of trustees got involved, and the state legislature, perish the thought, got involved.

Why was Auburn allowing state money (student activity fees) to be used so this liberal preacher from the North, this un-American, "pinkco" liberal, and, in all likelihood, a communist sympathizer, could speak at Auburn?

President Harry Philpott was caught in the middle of a gathering storm. He was in "a pickle," as old folks said in that day. As university administrators often are, he was damned if he did and damned if he didn't. Whatever he did was going to be wrong.

Ultimately he decided university funds of any type could not be used to pay for an appearance by anyone who openly advocated violating the law. That, of course, included Coffin. Some of the students and many of the faculty were appalled by his decision.

As editor of the *Auburn Plainsman*, I, against wishes of the staff, supported Philpott. Somebody was going to have to make a decision, I reasoned, and I much preferred the president make it rather than someone in Montgomery, namely someone in the state legislature, make it.

The students sponsoring the event contacted Morris Dees, now a distinguished civil rights attorney, and filed suit in federal court to allow Coffin to speak.

The case was heard in Judge Frank Johnson's courtroom. To this ole boy from small-town Alabama, it was quite unseemly, even disturbing, to see the college president sitting nervously on the witness stand being grilled by Dees and, on occasion, questioned by Judge Johnson.

I have never lost my high regard for Dr. Philpott and have come to admire, respect, and deeply appreciate Morris Dees and Judge Johnson. Alabama and the nation would be vastly different places were it not for their courage, their commitment, and their efforts.

Judge Johnson, of course, ruled in favor of the plaintiffs, and Rev. Coffin came and spoke at Auburn. It was no big deal. In the end, it was much ado about very little, except for the big issue of free speech.

In looking back on it, I have come to believe Dr. Philpott, President Philpott, was craftier than his critics may have thought.

There was no way he, in good conscience, could refuse or deny Coffin's right to speak and the students' right to hear him. But if he did so without putting up a fight, the state legislature's threat to cut funding to Auburn could have become a dangerous reality. That's the way state government under George Wallace and his cronies operated in those days.

But if the federal court ordered him to let Coffin speak, then he, Philpott, had the cover he needed with the board of trustees and the legislature. "I did all I could to stop it," he could truthfully say.

He never told me that was his strategy, but in later years, others close to him said that it was.

During all of this, on a Wednesday afternoon I believe it was, a group of student leaders staged what may have been the first student political protest at Auburn. With masking tape covering their mouths, student leaders carried a closed casket around Ross Square, stopped in front of Ross Hall, and declared "the death of free speech in Auburn." As editor, I ripped them pretty good in the next issue of the *Plainsman*.

But now, after all these years, to SGA president, Jimmy Bryan, Joe Busta, Phil Wallace, Sam Phillips, and others who were involved in that protest march, I apologize.

You were right; I was wrong. So wrong.

William Sloane Coffin should have been allowed to speak at Auburn without controversy. Freedom of speech covers all speech, even speech we don't like or agree with.

Safety concerns have to be addressed, of course, and the principle of free speech should not be used to justify rhetoric intended to disrupt and promote violence. Everything has its limits, like shouting "fire" in a crowded theater.

But a university, at its finest and best, should be a place where ideas, opinions, and beliefs can be openly discussed and debated without fear of threat or reprisal.

Perhaps I should be embarrassed by my earlier position on the Coffin affair, but I'm not.

I see it as a measure of how far I have come, as a person, a citizen, and as a defender of free speech.

I have not made this journey alone. Many of you have made it with me, this journey from where we were to where we are and ought to be. Age and experience continue to be great teachers.

In my ripening old age, I might not agree with what you say, and I might not like what you say, but I will defend to the end your right to say it.

If this makes me a liberal, then so be it. I wear that honor proudly.

Jack Howell

Jack Howell was a good man.

A quiet man but a good man, a good and strong man.

When he spoke, people listened and with good reason. His words and thoughts were worthy of notice and attention. He dispatched wisdom and leadership in a calm, soft-spoken manner. I never heard the words *mad* or *anger* associated with his name.

He was a kind and wise man, the kind of man you wanted to emulate when you grew up, to have the respect he had. Be like Jack Howell, and you will be a good man.

That may be the most significant compliment one could receive. "Mr. Jack" was worthy of it. He was that kind of man.

He made a difference for good in the small town where he was born, raised, and lived his entire life, and he made a difference in the lives of the people who shared that small town with him, especially the young people. Ever the encourager, he always had a warm smile and words of encouragement for young people just beginning to find their way in the world.

He was born on the farm and spent his entire life on

the farm, farming, raising a few cows, and managing a few chicken houses. He was used to work, hard work, and he was close to nature. Maybe that, in part, accounts for his wisdom and perspective.

My daddy used to tell the story, quite often really, about the time the church came up $100 short of its annual budget. That was back when $100 was a lot of money. "How much do we need?" Jack asked. When told the amount, he immediately wrote a check for $100. As long as he had the wherewithal to help, he was not about to let the church come up short. He was that kind of man.

He was an Auburn man and an Auburn fan, but he did stray. When his grandson walked on at Alabama and made the team, Jack could still love Auburn, but he had to support his grandson, even against Auburn. That's what he did in the Auburn-Alabama game of 2012. It was a painful, poignant day for Jack and his wife, Octavia, but when his grandson's playing days were over, Jack was back, 100 percent Auburn again.

Jack called the other day, said he was going to be in Auburn over the weekend and wanted to come by and say hello. As it turned out, he came to say goodbye.

He was bent, withered, and unsteady as he made his way into the house. I was shocked. He looked old, even for eighty-six, but his spirits were good, his wit quick, and his mind as strong as ever. We had a good visit, talking about the old days, old friends, and family, most of them gone. We rejoiced in their memory and laughed a bit too. It was a good Saturday.

When it came time to leave, Jack wanted to have our picture taken. Then we embraced and said, as all of us do when parting, "I'll be seeing you."

A day and a half later, early on a Monday morning, the call came. Jack had died in his sleep the night before.

One has to be careful when writing about premonitions, feelings or urgings of the spirit, but when we embraced that day, I think we both knew we would not see each other again this side of the veil. I saw it in his eyes. Jack had come to say goodbye, and I'm glad, even blessed, that he did.

Jack Howell never wrote a book, never had a street named for him, never ran for or held elective office as far as I know. He never did any of the things that the world would celebrate and acclaim as important, but he left this world, especially the small town where he lived, a better place. And the people in that town are better too. I am one of them.

Rest in peace, my friend, and thank you.

Thank you for being my friend, as a boy, and now, as a growing-older old man.

Thank you for setting an example for me to follow.

You made a difference in my life.

All Hail the Green Wave

All hail the Green Wave, State 3A Baseball Champions. Now, if the school could just get its spelling and grammar correct, they would have a great school.

GHS is already a good school, maybe a great school, but it persists and insists on being grammatically incorrect.

These new folks up there call themselves the "Greenwave." That's not right; that's wrong, very much wrong. That term is most likely a perpetuated spelling error brought about by a headline writer or a screen printer trying to make letters fit into a given space, a space too small for "Green Wave" but not too small for "Greenwave."

Other schools that use Green Wave as a mascot, Tulane and Leeds included, spell it as two words, not one. But not Gordo, not my beloved Gordo. The new folks up there persist on being grammatically incorrect and spelling it "Greenwave."

Anybody knows, ought to know, there's no such word or term as "greenwave." Check it out on spellcheck or in a dictionary.

There is, however, a strong tradition of "Green Wave."

Calling Gordo the "Greenwave" is like calling Alabama the Crimsontide or Auburn the Auburn Wareagles. It's just wrong, and though we have all made spelling errors from time to time, I hate to see my school persist in the same spelling error year after year. It's time to get it corrected, and what better time than after winning a state championship?

I know, I know, I'm just a crazy, cranky old man crying in the wilderness, but crying I am, and cry I will.

If you are going to have a great school, you ought to at least be able to spell the name of your mascot correctly. And it's "Green Wave," not "Greenwave."

Now this is sure to get the homefolks riled up a bit, I know, but right is right, and wrong is wrong.

After all, we want to have a school our state baseball champions can be proud of.

And that means knowing how to spell.

Jack Simms

Jack Simms was a good man.

As William Shakespeare wrote in *Julius Caesar*, "the elements so mixed in him that all the world might stand say, 'this was a man …'"

Jack Simms was such a man.

As a marine in some of the toughest, bloodiest, inch-by-inch, hand-to-hand fighting in the Pacific during World War II, he displayed his mettle, his toughness, and his courage again and again.

He once said his whole war was fought defending or trying to take the ten yards in front of him. In the trenches, on the front lines, it wasn't about patriotism or motherhood; it was about survival, your survival and the survival of the man, the friend, the buddy, next to you.

Marines are America's best, America's toughest, and Jack Simms was a marine, a proud marine. He wore the red coat of a marine veteran often and proudly.

Tom Brokaw talks about the "Greatest Generation." Jack Simms was part of that generation. Brokaw had men like Jack in mind when he coined the phrase Greatest Generation. He made the world safer during the war, and he made it better after the war. His war experiences did not define hm. They were only part of who he was.

He had a heart, a kindness and a compassion, that he did his best to hide.

He tried to, and often did, come across as a tough, strict disciplinarian, an academic marine drill sergeant of sort, but he had a heart, a big heart, as a reporter, as an editor, and as a professor.

It was as if he didn't want his students to know how much he cared for them, how much he loved them, until they graduated, and then he was their biggest supporter, their best friend, their greatest ally.

No professor, no department head, ever worked harder to find jobs and secure opportunities for his students than Jack did. He stayed in touch with them, most of them, for the rest of his life. He made a difference in their lives, and they enriched his life. It was a mutually beneficial experience.

He was a pillar in the university and in the community for whatsoever was right and good. He was a quiet leader, but his influence was strong, and it was effective.

At his Friday-morning breakfast club, he talked about issues and ideas, not people. When the talk turned to criticism of people, Jack became quiet. It was noted and appreciated. He was not a gossip as most, if not all, men are.

No matter what the subject, when Jack spoke, people listened. He had that kind of respect. He had the ability and wherewithal to disagree agreeably, a quality that is becoming more and more rare in these times in which we live.

When the subject of theology came up, which it often did, he would quietly and respectfully listen to others' opinions and beliefs. He would sometimes discreetly turn away, rolling his eyes in disbelief that anybody could see life, the world, and faith that way, but he never tried to convince them that they should believe as he believed. He didn't talk or argue his faith. He lived it, and he lived it well.

Lest we forget, Jack was human too.

Nobody loved a party more than Jack; the more, the merrier. He enjoyed a good, stiff drink (or drinks), and he could tell a story. Oh, how he could tell a story. He was Auburn's best. He loved to have a good time. He loved life and all that it entailed.

A strong man, a courageous man, a tough man. That was Jack Simms. A kind man, a caring man, a compassionate and respectful man, and a man of faith. That was Jack Simms.

Jack Simms was a good man. I was blessed to work for him and even more blessed to have him as my friend.

He was a great American.

A Debt of Gratitude

Summer is here again, and as the years go by, I think more and more about a Gordo teacher—a librarian—who made a difference in my life.

Back in the early to midfifties, sixty or more years ago, "Miss" Ruth Junkin, later to become Ruth Holliman, introduced me to the joys of reading.

I was in elementary school and always looking for something to do in the summer. (There were only two television channels then, and they weren't on all day, so what's a boy to do?)

She volunteered to come to school once a week at a designated hour and let me check out books from the library.

Through her kindness, I was introduced to all kinds of people who went before me: presidents, generals, patriots, and pioneers. I was able to be there as historical events that shaped our nation and the world took place, and through reading, I have traveled many places, both far and near, places I have never been to personally but places that came to me through the written word and the mind's eye.

I owe all of that to her and to her willingness to help a

young boy read and learn through the summer. Reading has made all the difference in my life, and I give her much of the credit for recognizing and encouraging that interest at a young age.

As another summer comes, I think about her and wish I could somehow thank her again.

In the Beginning

I came to Auburn fifty-two years ago today, June 9, 1965. It was one of the three most important days of my life. The first is October 18, 1946, the day I was born; the second, June 15, 1985, is the day I got married. The first gave me life; the second changed that life forever.

All of my life, for as long as I could remember, all I ever really wanted to do was to come to Auburn and be a part of Auburn.

Yet, on that long ago day as I watched that used black Ford Fairlane drive to the top of Thach Avenue and disappear beyond the Presbyterian church, I'll never forget the feeling that came over me.

I had what I had always wanted, my dream had come true, but now with Momma and Daddy gone, I was uncertain. Not scared; uncertain. Not sure if I would make it, not sure if I could make it.

My first Auburn meal was at the Kopper Kettle, the only place I knew to eat. There would be many more meals in that little diner on the corner of Gay and Magnolia, most of them late-night meals, late, late, late-night meals.

I shall never forget that first night in Auburn. I was the only person in a makeshift six-room rooming house. Each student had his own room. None of the others had moved in, and I was alone, as alone as I had ever been in my life. My old life had passed away, and I wasn't sure what this new life might hold.

I straightened the room, organized the dresser, arranged what few clothes I had brought from home, none of them stylish enough for college, in the closet, and positioned my study lamp on a scarred wooden table. The room was sparse, Spartan sparse. What else could you expect for fifty dollars a quarter?

I made up the bed—a cot that served as a bed—and lay down to think about what might be ahead.

Could an overweight boy with a speech impediment make it at Auburn? Could a boy from a small-town Alabama high school make it at a big school like Auburn? Would I be able to make friends? Could I find my way, would I find my way, and where would that way lead?

All of those fears, cares, and anxieties raced through my teenage mind and heart on that night so long ago.

Then, at midnight, I heard the bells of Samford Tower chime for the first time, their rich, strong, baritone sounds signaling the changing of the day, from one day to the next, from the old to the new, a new beginning.

John Wesley talks about his heart feeling strangely warmed at Aldersgate.

My heart was strangely warmed at 219 East Thach in Auburn, Alabama, as June 9 turned to June 10 in 1965.

Suddenly, my fears, anxieties, and uncertainties were gone. I was at Auburn. I was home. All was well, and all would be well.

Thank God for the bells of Samford Tower. They continue to be a source of strength and sustenance, a constant reminder of that night so long ago when it all came together, when it all became real, when my new life began.

The next day, I went to the *Plainsman* office and volunteered, then to the Athletic Department and volunteered to work in the Sports Publicity Office, as it was called in those days.

The rest, as they say, is history, and my life has never been the same.

I am a totally different person from the one I was on that day so long ago. I—we—should be different as we grow, learn, and begin to think for ourselves, as we become the people we are destined to be.

The basic sense of right and wrong is still there, but the world has become complicated, much more complicated than I could have ever imagined—more complicated than any of us could have imagined.

I came here with a strong faith, and it is still strong but in different ways. As a fellow traveler so wisely said, "The older I get the fewer beliefs I have, but the more I believe." A lot of things I used to believe were true I no longer believe to be true, but my faith is deeper and more meaningful than ever before.

The only thing that teenage boy of so long ago wanted was to be a part of Auburn and to make it better. I like to think he did, that I did, but only time will tell. Time judges all things.

I am no longer on the front lines of the fight for all that is good and true about Auburn. I am an elder statesman now, and that's the way it should be, the old giving way to the young. Life was planned that way, and it is good.

As MacArthur said, "Old soldiers never die, they just fade away …" That young boy of long ago is now an old soldier, a veteran of many Auburn wars, fading away slowly and, I hope, gracefully.

As my Auburn years fade into the twilight, I go forward with only one hope. It is the same hope that has driven me all of my life.

I hope I've made a difference. At Auburn, yes, but more importantly I hope I've made a difference in the lives of young people. On a college campus, in a college town, that's the only thing that matters.

It is the only thing of lasting value.

June 9, 1965 mattered.

It still matters.

I Wish He Hadn't Said It

Dan Rather, I'm talking about.

I wish he hadn't said it, but it's true. And sometimes, the truest things hurt the most.

It was the days after 9-11, the shock of it all still very much in evidence, the moving-on process not yet beginning.

Dan Rather was being interviewed on one of those late-night talk shows, I forget which one, and it really doesn't matter. What he said mattered then, and it matters still. I just wish he hadn't said it, at least not the way he said it.

With the lights of the World Trade Center recovery site and its still smoking ruins in the background, Rather was asked what this attack meant to the country, how it would affect us, our psyche, going forward in the days, weeks, months, and years to come.

"It's now evident," he said, "that we can no longer count on the width of oceans to protect us from our enemies as it has throughout our history. War has come to our shores, to our homeland. We know now that we are vulnerable as we've never been before …"

Then he said the words that continue to bring sadness to the depths of my being.

With deep emotion, this hardened, veteran newsman who had seen the best and now the worst said, "We'll never be able to sing 'America the Beautiful' the same way again ... not that part about 'alabaster cities gleam undimmed by human tears ...' We can't say that anymore." He fought back tears as he spoke.

I think about Dan Rather's words quite often, riding around Auburn, driving to Birmingham, reading a book, listening to music, watching the Yankees or Jordan Spieth on TV, or just doing nothing. His words come to mind again and again. They haunt me, always bringing sadness with them. Always. *"We can never sing that song the same way again ..."*

Why, you may ask, are we talking about this in the week leading up to the Fourth of July, a time for great celebration and patriotism?

Last Sunday at Auburn United Methodist Church's Star-Spangled Spectacular, a wonderful patriotic celebration of our country, the first song was "America the Beautiful." The choir and the congregation burst forth singing Katharine Lee Bates's moving, stirring words once again.

Then came the fourth stanza, and those words—those words—were there again, as always: "thine alabaster cities gleam, undimmed by human tears." I had to stop singing.

It all came back again, that second plane making the

slow but sure turn into the South Tower, the explosion that followed, the smoke, the fire, men and women jumping to their deaths rather than await the inevitable, people, our panic-stricken fellow citizens, running through the streets of Lower Manhattan trying to escape the cloud of dust and debris that pursued and threatened to overwhelm them.

We lost our innocence that day. As Dan Rather said, we were protected by the oceans no longer, and our cities no longer undimmed by human tears. We had become vulnerable.

In thinking about all of this over the last few days, I have come to the conclusion that it is better, far better, to have an impregnable resilience than a false sense of impregnable security.

Resiliency, not a false sense of security, is the key to our well-being and to our future, as individuals, as a people, and as a country.

Resilience. It is the difference between cast iron and tempered steel. Cast iron, a false sense of security, will shatter into pieces. Tempered steel, forged steel, is stronger and more lasting. Its resiliency gives it strength to endure, strength to carry on. Resiliency.

The story of 9-11 didn't end when the towers came down. It continues today with wars, police actions, and battles against evil all over the world.

But what has become the most enduring symbol of 9-11 is

a tall building dominating the skyline of Lower Manhattan as the World Trade Center once did.

It's called Freedom Tower. It represents the resilience of our nation and its people, the firemen and policemen who courageously and fearlessly rushed to help that day and our fellow citizens who ran for their lives that day.

Freedom Tower exists, most especially, to assure the sons and daughters, the wives and husbands, the parents and grandparents, the friends who lost loved ones that day that their loss is not destined to be forgotten.

Dan Rather was right. I have never sung and will never sing, "America the Beautiful" the same way again. Those words, that phrase, "thine alabaster cities gleam undimmed by human tears," still bring a soreness to my soul and a tightness to my throat, just as it brought an emotional Dan Rather to tears on that night so long ago.

But as the line passes, I think about another hymn, a psalm actually, the one that says, "Joy cometh in the morning …"

It always will. With resilience and faith, the real and lasting strengths of our country and its people, we will endure. And we will continue to be the United States of America.

I find great comfort in that.

Memories of the Fourth of July

A long time ago ...

More watermelons than a boy could count floating in a barrel of ice ...

More soft drinks than a boy could comprehend in their own barrel of ice, Cokes, Bubble Ups, Grapico and Nehi Orange, a dime a piece. Mr. Adolph Sanders ...

Do they make Bubble Up anymore, Coca-Cola's answer to 7-Up?

Pink lemonade by the barrel. It was the only time we ever saw pink lemonade ...

The greased pig chase. Catch the pig and win twenty dollars ...

The greased pole contest. Climb the greased pole and get the money on top. Each climber was allowed three tries ...

Great fun. Great, great fun. Grease was a popular thing in my hometown ...

Tons and tons of barbecue served in the school lunchroom. Seventy-five cents a plate ...

Woodrow Sims and the Gordo Eagles taking on all comers in a doubleheader that afternoon. All games had to end before nightfall. No lights in those days ...

Not wanting the fading twilight to come ...

Everyone in town making their way home when it did ...

Members of the Lions Club, sponsor of the event, cleaning up, talking about what a great day it had been ...

All that talk in the shade, political and otherwise, without a voice being raised in anger. Those were the days ...

Not much talk about patriotism or the Declaration of Independence, but we knew why we were there ...

A long time ago in a galaxy far, far away ...

I am glad I got to experience it all ...

If that's not the way it was, it's the way I remember it, and that's good enough for me ...

The Letter G

It came in a brown, padded envelope a day or two ago from an address I did not recognize.

It turned out to be one of the nicest, kindest, most thoughtful gestures one could ever receive.

Inside was a T-shirt commemorating my ole high school's recent state championship in baseball and a note. It was the note that got me:

> Mr. Housel,
> On behalf of my teammates and I, I would like to thank you for your support throughout my high school career. I hope my classmates & I have done our part to carry on the winning "Green Wave" tradition the right way.
>
> I will be attending Shelton State to play baseball. My goal is to one day play baseball on the Plains for the Tigers.
>
> I hope this card finds you & yours well and that you will wear this shirt with pride.

> From one generation of Green Wave to another, Roll Wave Roll!
>
> Sincerely,
> Koy Chapman #7
> And, of course, WDGW!

Koy Chapman played shortstop on the state championship baseball team and quarterback on three Green Wave (and he spelled it right, "Green Wave," not "Greenwave") teams that compiled a 39–3 record and came within a whisper of winning the state football championship all three years.

To my knowledge, I've never met the young man, but I have admired and appreciated his work from afar. I hope he is as good a person as he is an athlete.

I have no reason to think he is not.

There was only one way to respond to a letter like that. I went to the boxed-up memories of my past. Coach Jordan and Coach Beard shared their mementos with me. Now it was time for me to do the same.

My response to young Mr. Chapman:

> Dear Koy,
> Thank you for your kind, generous and thoughtful note. I will wear the state championship shirt with pride, and I will wear it to the Backbooth at Chappy's where I can

boast and brag on you guys and the Green Wave a little more.

Your note moved me. It is obvious that you have an understanding and appreciation of pride and tradition that pass from generation to generation.

In thinking about how to respond to your note, I could think of only one appropriate way.

Enclosed you will find my varsity letter "G" from 52 years ago. I want you to have it.

It has meant a lot to me over the years as a tangible symbol of one of the most memorable, formative, and enjoyable times of my life.

When I am no longer here, it would most likely have been discarded as most personal mementoes are. Others, no matter how much they love you, can't understand or appreciate why certain little things mean so much. I believe you can, and that's why I want you to have it.

And who knows, 52 years from now you may pass this on to your grandson. Tell him it belonged to a guy who played tackle on the 1964 Green Wave, the greatest Green Wave team ever. (That may not be true—you were on some pretty good teams yourself—but that's the way we old guys like to remember it.)

Best wishes, my young friend, in all of your endeavors and in all that you do. I hope your dreams of playing baseball at Auburn come true.

And, yes, WDGW*, yes, War Eagle!

David Housel

*War Damn Green Wave

Kudzu and Football

Football practice has started. Yaaa-hoooo!

In the old days, football practice started September 1; September 1 for everyone, no exceptions.

Now practice starts in July.

Football is like kudzu. It just keeps creeping and creeping, earlier and earlier.

In the days when practice started the first day of September, the season started the last Saturday in September. Each team had three to four weeks to practice, depending on the calendar.

If both teams agreed, as Alabama and Georgia did in 1960, their first game could be played the third week of September, allowing about two weeks—in this case, sixteen days—to prepare. Sixteen days, an unheard of thing today.

Why did Alabama and Georgia agree to play a week early? Then, as now, the reason was television.

Now practice starts in July, and the season starts the last week in August. No, Auburn and Alabama don't play that first week of the season, but they could. Other teams do.

Football, a game meant to be played in the fall, like kudzu, just keeps creeping and creeping, toward the heart and heat of summer. Where it will stop nobody knows.

We've all heard people say, more and more often it seems, "I can't wait for football season to start," or "I wish football season started tomorrow." They'd best be careful. They are wishing their lives away.

As we near the end of our lives, we will wish we could get back all of those days we wiled away wishing and waiting for something as inconsequential as the start of football season.

Football season will come when it will come. It is up to us to live each day to its fullest, football or no football.

How It All Began

One hundred and twenty-five years ago tonight, a group of young men, students and professors from Alabama Mechanical College (AMC), later to be known as Auburn, were in Atlanta celebrating a 10–0 victory over the University of Georgia in the start of what was to become the oldest and longest football rivalry in the Deep South and one of the longest in the nation.

George Petrie, a mild-mannered history and Latin professor, was Auburn's first coach. The game had come about because of his deep friendship with Dr. Charles Herty at Georgia.

Both had discovered the new game of "foot ball" at Johns Hopkins and brought it back to their respective campuses when their graduate work was over.

Their teams had been practicing for six months when Auburn challenged Georgia to an inevitable game to see who was better, Petrie and Auburn or Herty and Georgia. The game was set for Atlanta's Piedmont Park as part of a celebration of George Washington's birthday. It was the first real game of foot ball played in the South.

Petrie made his twenty-one players sign an oath that they would not partake of alcohol on the trip to Atlanta to ensure they wouldn't run the risk of embarrassing the college.

They may or may not have had a drink, but they certainly didn't embarrass their school. AMC, now Auburn, has celebrated their exploits ever since. A small, loving cup, given to the winner by the J.P. Stephens Company of Atlanta, is proudly displayed in Auburn's athletics museum even unto this day.

Unsure of how many people would come to the game, Petrie and the team, which included Cliff Hare, for whom Auburn's stadium would be named, rode the streetcar from the Kimball House, headquarters hotel for both teams, to Piedmont Park where an estimated five thousand fans, an unheard of number in that day, awaited.

Admission was fifty cents for adults, a quarter for children, and a dollar for a carriage space. According to Clyde Bolton, in his wonderful book, *War Eagle—The Story of Auburn Football*, gate receipts were only $800. The crowd had to have been evangelistically overestimated, or a lot people sneaked in without paying.

Auburn's mascot, according to Clyde, was Dabble, a large boy who wore bright orange trousers, a spike-tailed blue coat, and a white sash. Georgia's mascot was a goat, Sir William, that wore a black coat with "U.G." in red on the side.

The boys from AMC wore white canvas jackets, white

padded trousers, orange belts, blue stockings, and white caps trimmed in blue. Georgia wore white uniforms, red caps, and black stockings.

Uniforms were rather expensive by standards of that day. Canvas jackets cost $1.50, padded pants, $2.25, and hose, fifty cents. Petrie had to borrow money to pay for the uniforms.

The favorite cheer of AMC fans who had come to Atlanta by train that same day was "Rah ra ree, Rah ra ree, Alabama A-M-C" or, for some, the earthier, "Shoot the Billy goat!"

After a scoreless first half, the recovery of a fumbled punt led to a short touchdown run by AMC's Dutch Dorsey. Sometime later, Jesse Culver picked up another fumbled punt near midfield and returned it for an AMC touchdown. Turnovers mattered, even then.

Touchdowns counted four points in those days, extra points, two. Auburn kicked the first extra point, missed the second, and won the game 10–0.

In later years, Petrie would write, "I had many happy moments in my life, but not often, if ever, have I been as happy as I as when that game was over.

"Many staid and perfectly sober citizens in the grandstands acted like crazy youngsters. One charming and gentle lady from Auburn, in her excitement, broke her parasol over the head and shoulders of a gentleman in front of her whom she had never seen before."

It got better (or worse, depending on your perspective)

as players and fans of both schools gathered at the Kimball House to celebrate the game and the day, the first of what they hoped would become a long-standing tradition in years to come.

The *Atlanta Journal* would later note, "On occasions with such hilarity as this, there are always some who will imbibe too freely. Those individuals were not wanting in the Kimball rotunda Saturday night. There was a varied assortment of drunks, and they were the most ridiculous drunks at that. There was the loud, irrepressible jag and the quite, droll drunk, the fighting drunk and the affectionate drunk. One enthusiast spent the entire evening cursing an imaginary policeman …"

There were, no doubt, sober fans in attendance that night, the AMC foot ball team presumably among them.

That's the way it was, February 20, 1892, when college football came to the South for the first time.

The South has never been the same.

O.C. Brown

1936–2017

O.C. Brown is one of the most important people in my life.

At a time when I might have been prone to wander, he was my rock, my anchor. He kept me close to the faith.

The year was 1965, and a small-town college freshman was beginning to wonder about it all. Was it really true, or were those things I had heard and been taught in Sunday school and church just stories and myths to keep children and young people from going astray?

Church seemed so far away, so irrelevant. My childhood faith was wandering, perhaps even slipping.

Then came O.C. Brown.

Word spread across campus that there was a dynamic young preacher at a small, little-known church called Grace Church located on Glenn Avenue, out beyond Glendean Gulf and Gleandean Drugs.

For reasons known only to God, I decided to check it out, and my life has never been the same.

The word "Gospel" is supposed to mean "good news," and the preacher, that O.C. Brown, made it good news, celebratory news. He gave me reason to go to church and to give the faith of my childhood another chance.

O.C. brought an air of anticipation and expectation to the Gospel. Grace Church was the most exciting, joyful place to be in Auburn. He made the Gospel real, and he made it relevant in my life and in the lives of the people who heard him, especially the young people. It was as if we were hearing the Gospel for the first time. And perhaps we were, the real Gospel.

Through his energetic, caring, and compassionate style, the humor and pathos of the human heart that he understood and conveyed so well, he assured us that the values and truths we had been told were real were, indeed, real.

Through his wit, his humor, and his conversational ease of style, he made the old new and touched our hearts, our minds, and our souls.

There was not a seat to be had in Grace Church in those days. His sermons—his thoughts—were piped into every room in the church. Every chair was taken. Every hallway filled.

He made a difference, and when you make a difference in a college town, you never know how far your influence will spread. Like ripples in a still body of water, it goes on and on.

The difference O.C. made spread far and wide. I am but one example.

We stayed semi-in-touch over the years. I always knew he was there for me. I watched in horror and in sorrow as he endured the physical and emotional pains of a modern-day Job. He handled them as well as any mortal could. He was not always strong, but he was never weak.

Though handicapped and severely crippled, he never lost his sense of humor or that always-present twinkle in his eyes. He never lost the thought that he could still make a difference, now through his letters to the editors of local and state newspapers.

He was often a voice of conscience in the community. Every community needs a conscience.

His lasting contribution will be in the influence he had on people, especially young people, the Auburn students of fifty or more years ago.

I am blessed to be one of them.

Whatever man I become, whatever good I may do, I owe in large part to O.C. Brown.

He will live in my heart forever.

Iron Mike

A convincing argument could be made that Mike Donahue was the best and greatest coach in the history of Auburn football. A strong argument.

There is no doubt that he is the single most influential person in Auburn's athletics history. No doubt at all about that. But first, the football.

Consider these words from Zipp Newman, longtime sports editor of the *Birmingham News* and an even longer observer of southern football:

> Auburn had an enrollment of 200. Donahue didn't have five high schools in Alabama to draw on for players. He had no coaching staff, recruiters, football game pictures—and there were rocks on the practice field.
>
> Mike Donahue had to take small boys, tall and gangling farm boys, and teach them to play a 'strange' game—hiking, the tactic of carrying, hurtling, or pushing the ball carrier as far as possible.

> The outstanding characteristics of Mike Donahue's teams were being ready, having courage, confidence, clean play, and fine sportsmanship. Donahue was a thorough fundamentalist. He believed defense won, and he believed in playing students and playing by the code of ethics.
>
> Donahue was first a father and then a coach to his boys. He took many poor boys from their farms and hamlets—not only making fine football players out of them—but guiding them into successful accomplishments in business. Donahue was the Auburn Spirit—he was the War Eagle!

Donahue's teams won ninety-nine games from 1904–06 and 1908–1922. This was in a time when teams played only seven or eight games a year.

When he came to Auburn, people wondered if he could coach. He didn't look like a coach. Born in Ireland, he stood five four, had red hair and blue eyes, and people could hardly understand a word he said. Yet, not long after his Auburn career began, he was known throughout the football world as "Iron Mike."

He would have three undefeated seasons, and seven of his eighteen teams would lose one game or less.

The eleven years between 1908 and 1919 were, and may continue to be, the halcyon days of Auburn football. Donahue's teams won three conference championships and a national championship (1913), had six seasons with one or no losses, and had a defense that shut out twenty-one of twenty-three opponents in a 22–0–1 run. Not bad for a team that had rocks on its practice field.

The 1913–1914 teams may have been the best in Auburn history. They were certainly the most impressive, winning sixteen of seventeen games. The 1914 Tigers didn't allow a point the entire season and beat the Carlisle Indians, a power at the time, 7–0 in Atlanta.

Little wonder that Ed Danforth of the *Atlanta Journal* wrote, "You were nobody until you had beaten Auburn. That was the place card for the head table."

Donahue's greatest player, the Bo Jackson of his day, was a wee little quarterback named Kirk Newell, captain of the 1913 national championship team. To keep the team in shape, Donahue would give Newell, nicknamed "Rabbit," a five-yard head start and then tell the rest of the team to catch him as he ran across campus. They seldom, if ever, did.

There can be no doubt that Donahue contributed more to Auburn's athletics program than any person who ever lived.

As Auburn's first athletics director, he added basketball for men and women, baseball, and track to Auburn's athletics program. And he coached all four teams in addition to his football responsibilities.

It is altogether fitting and proper that Donahue Drive, which runs through the heart of Auburn's athletic facilities, be named in his memory.

A worthy tribute to a man who might be called the first "Mr. Auburn."

Iron Mike Donahue

The Forgotten Man

The ravages of time have made him an almost forgotten man. Ask almost any Auburn fan today, "Who was Kirk Newell?" and most would likely shrug and say "Who?"

But Kirk Newell was one of the greatest men and greatest athletes ever to play at Auburn. The Bo Jackson of his day? That and much more. Kirk Newell did things Bo and Cam never did and, thankfully, were never called upon to do.

Through Jason Peevy's excellent work for Auburn's football centennial celebration, we know that Kirk Newell grew up in Dadeville and learned to run by chasing rabbits.

After his football days were over, his coach, the great Mike Donahue, had Newell come to practice, whereupon Donahue would engage the team in a drill he called "Try to Catch Kirk." Donahue said his players looked like a pack of dogs chasing a rabbit, noting that it was the best, most fun conditioning drill he had.

One sportswriter described Newell as "the greatest broken field runner in college football." But speed was not his only asset; he had power too. In a game against Vanderbilt, then considered the Alabama of its day, Newell picked up a fumble and returned it thirty-five yards for a touchdown.

It was not what he did but how he did it that was so impressive. As one Birmingham sportswriter wrote the next day: "Spunky little Mr. Newell bounced a couple of heavy Commodores out of the way, plunged under the third one and sent him toppling with a well-directed shoulder shove, seized the pigskin and with but 12 inches lead outran them for the goal. He displayed brains, speed and general football ability."

He stood five feet seven inches tall, weighed 145 pounds, and was nicknamed "The Runt." That referred to his size, but because of his talent and leadership ability, he might well have been known as "The Giant," as Peevy notes.

Just how big was that touchdown? It was Auburn's first touchdown against Vanderbilt in sixteen years. Auburn had not beaten Vanderbilt in twenty years, but with Kirk Newell at the helm, all of that was about to change.

He was quarterback of Auburn's undefeated 1913 team, which won the Southern Championship and was later named National Champion by the Billingsley rating system. That team, even now, is arguably the greatest Auburn football team of all time.

With Newell at the helm as captain and playing both offense and defense, Donahue's Tigers scored 223 points in eight games and gave up only thirteen points, six to Vanderbilt in a 12–6 victory in Birmingham and seven to Georgia in a

21–7 win in Atlanta. The Georgia game was a classic of its day, undefeated Auburn against undefeated Georgia, winner take all, and Auburn took it all, the Southern Championship and, some say, the national championship.

"The Runt" gained 1,707 yards rushing as a senior in 1913 and averaged 213 yards rushing a game, something even the great Bo Jackson was not able to do. Who was the best player? The best runner? It is impossible to say—two different styles, two different times, decades apart. Who can ever say—say for sure?

Newell had never seen a football until he came to Auburn. Baseball was his game, as it was Bo's favorite game. But Mike Donahue knew an athlete when he saw one, and before Newell's career was complete, he had lettered in football, baseball, basketball, track, and soccer. Auburn's greatest athlete? Again, who can tell, who can ever know, and how is greatness truly defined other than to say the greatest of his or her era?

But there were qualities about Newell, character, leadership, and a concern for others, that transcended athletic fields and athletic competition. While training recruits how to throw hand grenades out of trenches in World War I, Newell was severely injured when one of his trainees panicked, dropped his grenade in the trench, and ran rather than throwing it as he had been instructed to do.

Sensing the danger to his men, Newell fell on the grenade,

taking the brunt of the explosion himself. Two men died, but Newell, scarred and mangled, miraculously survived and went on to a successful career as a pharmacist in Birmingham.

Kirk Newell—a man worth remembering, now and forever.

And especially on this, the one hundredth anniversary of his greatest season.

Kirk Newell

On Aging

For some reason, I got to thinking about Mr. Troy Johnson's barbershop on the way home from church today.

I remember as a kid needing help to get into the barber's chair. I barely remember it, but I do remember it.

Now that I am old, I need help again.

Such is life.

The Man

Let's get the sad stuff, the unfortunate stuff, out of the way first. For a person of my generation, a child of the sixties, it is hard to say this, but it is nonetheless true. Truth telling is often hard.

Coach Ralph "Shug" Jordan, forever my Auburn coach and the man who defines Auburn football for my generation, could not survive today. That is not so much a comment on him as it is about the times in which we live.

Coach Jordan was head coach at Auburn for twenty-five years and won 176 games over those twenty-five years, an average of seven games a year. Not enough by today's standards.

Of course they only played ten games a year in those days. Extrapolating his winning percentage to today's twelve-game schedule, he would win about eight games a year. Not enough to survive in these times.

But those were different times, and Shug Jordan was a different kind of man, a different kind of coach.

At that time, many, if not most, successful coaches met

with their stock brokers at lunch during the season. Not Coach Jordan. He went home, at that time 185 Woodfield Drive, and had a sandwich with his wife.

It was never about money with Coach Jordan. The most he ever made from Auburn was $32,500 a year. In his last year of coaching, 1975, his television show and endorsement rights earned another $10,000. That was a goal for him, to him a measure of success. He wouldn't have gotten that if it were not for the dogged determination and loving efforts of Phil Snow, Carl Stephens, and Buddy Davidson.

The winningest coach in Auburn history earning $42,500 a year. My, how times have changed.

He was of the old school. That's why Auburn people were patient and tolerant when his teams didn't compete for the championship every year. He was one of them, class of '32, and they loved it. Every Thursday night before a big game, he and his wife, Evelyn, ate supper at the Grille, adjacent to Toomer's Corner. A tradition was born.

He never met a stranger, and he took time to talk with everyone, no matter how big, how small, whatever their station in life may be. It was not uncommon to see him walking in downtown Auburn or walking the dogs on Woodfield Drive. He was a man, a coach, of the people.

Sportswriters used to say interviewing Coach Jordan was like sitting down and visiting with your grandfather. In earlier years, the comparison had been visiting with your favorite uncle. He always made sure each reporter had a different angle, something all his own, something that made the reporter feel that he had a scoop.

He had what the Auburn Creed calls "the human touch," a touch of humanity "which cultivates sympathy with my fellow men and mutual helpfulness and brings happiness to all."

Winning was important, very important, to Coach Jordan, but it was not the only or most important thing. He kept football in perspective. How could he not keep it in perspective after having been in the lead Allied invasions of North Africa, Sicily, and France in World War II? He was wounded on Utah Beach in the early hours of D-Day and was awarded the Purple Heart. When the war ended, his unit was preparing for the invasion of Japan.

How could he not keep football in perspective?

He was known for his gentlemanly demeanor, but Alf Van Hoose, sports editor of the *Birmingham News*, unmasked him: "Coach Jordan comes across as a southern gentleman with his smile and ready handshake, but underneath there is an iron will, and a fist of steel, especially when it comes to football."

He was left-handed. Those who played or worked for him knew when that left arm started moving up and down with that left index finger pointed, something was about to happen. "The Man," as he was called, was making a point, and you had best listen. Listen and heed.

He believed in the value of work, hard work, as described in the Auburn Creed. That work ethic enabled him to turn the morass Auburn football had become into a championship contender in three years and win the national championship in six years.

When he came to Auburn, the stadium that was to later bear his name had a seating capacity of 21,500. When he retired, it had a capacity of 64,000. More than half of the seats in today's Jordan-Hare Stadium were added during his era.

He had his "Seven D's of Success: Discipline, Desire to Excel, Determination, Dedication, Dependability, Desperation and Damn it anyway, do something." They served him well in his day, as they serve us well today, in any day, in any form of human endeavor, especially in football.

He had a warm, self-deprecating humor. When he was introduced as the winningest football coach in Auburn history, he would sometimes chuckle and add, "But I'm the losingest too!"

Longevity has its rewards. Its risks too. Twenty-five years covers a lot of football games. He won 176, lost eighty-three, and tied six.

His record speaks for itself. It will be remembered for as long as football is played on the Plains. That is the nature of numbers.

But let's not forget the man.

Therein lay his greatness, his goodness, and his greatest contribution to Auburn.

Shug Jordan '32

Auburn Man

The Man

Passing the Torch

As we commemorate the 125th year of Auburn football, a quote from John F. Kennedy comes to mind again and again: "The Torch is passed to a New Generation ..."

That is happening here, today. The Auburn torch is beginning its journey to a new generation.

Return with us now to January 10, 2010, Glendale, Arizona. Auburn is playing Oregon for the national championship.

Two seconds to play, game tied 19–19, Auburn lining up to kick a nineteen-yard field goal. Number 19, Neil Caudle, is the holder. If you believe in astrology or horoscopy, the study of the future by the alignment of the planets and stars, it was all there: 19-19-19-19. There, in the stars.

Wes Byrum kicked it true. Neil Caudle's hands were the last Auburn hands, the last Auburn flesh, to touch the football before Auburn won the national championship. There is something special in that. The last Auburn hands, the last Auburn flesh ...

Now, return to today where the Auburn torch, as it has done for more than one hundred years, begins its journey from one generation to another.

Neil Caudle graduated, went to work for Brasfield-Gorrie in Birmingham, and married his Auburn sweetheart, Emily Amari.

They bought a home on a tree-lined street in Homewood and began their lives together, and good, happy lives they were.

Their lives got better and a lot busier last October when twins, Kate and Joe, joined the family. Kate and Joe took their first steps a few weeks ago. Life was good and getting better.

That brings us to today and the Auburn torch.

Kate and Joe are here today seeing and experiencing their first Auburn football game. Neil and Emily have planned this trip as a family trip all the way, bringing their children to Auburn, where their parents met, fell in love, studied, learned, and made their future alma mater better by their presence here.

And along the way, Neil helped Auburn win the national championship, its first in fifty-three years. Those last Auburn hands …

Kate and Joe will little note nor long remember any of what they see, hear, and experience here today, but it is a start, their start, to a life of Auburn and Auburn football, with all its thrills, chills, triumphs, disappointments, and all the unexpected vagaries in between.

Take it from us who have traveled this road, Auburn football is quite a journey, especially if it is filled with passion, as every worthwhile journey should be. Get ready, Kate, Joe. It's going to be a heck of a ride. If you were older, I would say "helluva" ride but, given your age, "heck of a" ride will have to do.

It has been suggested to Neil and Emily that they save the ticket stubs, a game program for each, and copies of tomorrow's *Birmingham News*, their hometown newspaper.

Put those keepsakes in a box, one for Joe, one for Kate, and hide those boxes safely away. Then one day, twenty, twenty-five, or thirty years from now, take that ticket stub, that program, and that newspaper and tell your children, "This is where your Auburn journey began, October 1, 2017."

May it be a good journey, a very good journey.

For them and for Auburn.

War Eagle!

War Eagle, forever!

The Caudle Family

Anything Can Happen Day

The original *Mickey Mouse Club*, the show from back in the fifties had a day called "Anything Can Happen Day"—on Wednesdays I believe it was. Anything could and did happen.

It was kind of like going to an Auburn football game. Anything can happen.

Kick Six.

The Prayer in Jordan-Hare.

Blocked punts

Unusual plays and colorful personalities have been part of Auburn football since the very beginning, back in 1892, when Frank Upton gained five yards running up the middle behind the Flying Wedge formation on the first offensive play in Auburn history.

Here are but a few:

- John Heisman's "Hidden Ball" play against Vanderbilt in 1895. With the team gathered around him, "Wee

Reynolds" Tichenor put the ball under his jersey. The team ran one way; he ran the other, sixty yards, untouched for a touchdown. Heisman ran the play again against Georgia. This time, Harry Smith hid the ball, and he, too, ran untouched for a touchdown.

- Heisman, for whom the Heisman Trophy is named, pioneered the center snap when centers began tossing or pitching the ball to the backs instead of rolling it back on the ground. He also devised the long snap count designed to draw the defensive team off sides.
- In 1894, again under Heisman's coaching, Auburn did not allow Georgia Tech to run a single offensive play the entire second half of a 94–0 loss. In those days, instead of kicking off, the scoring team got the ball back. Georgia Tech could never stop Auburn; hence, the Jackets didn't get to run a single play.
- Auburn accomplished a similar feat in 2006 when it did not allow South Carolina to run an offensive play in the third quarter. Auburn received the second-half kickoff, began a long, time-consuming touchdown drive, and then recovered an onside kick to get the ball back again. That later resulted in an Auburn score on the first play of the fourth quarter.
- In 1916, Richard "Moon" Ducote used his helmet as a tee in kicking a forty-five-yard field goal. Georgia protested mightily, but there was no rule against it, so

the field goal was allowed, resulting in a 3–0 Auburn victory.

- On November 10, 1934, in a prelude to what would happen thirty-eight years later on December 2, 1972, Auburn blocked two punts against Georgia Tech and returned them both for touchdowns. Mutt Mullins recovered the first blocked punt in the end zone for a touchdown. Haygood Paterson blocked the second punt and returned it twenty yards for Auburn's final touchdown in an 18–6 victory. Punt, Tech, punt!
- In 1953, after three quarters, Auburn trailed Mississippi State in Starkville 21–0. The State players seemed to know everything Auburn was going to do. Auburn coaches figured out—or thought—their phone lines to the sideline had been tapped. They stopped using the phones in the fourth quarter, and Auburn scored three straight touchdowns to tie a game that seemed hopelessly lost.
- 17-16 and Gary Sanders's call in the 1972 Alabama game: "It is blocked! It is blocked! It's caught on the run! He's gonna score!" giving rise to the now immortal "Punt, Bama, Punt."
- During the 1994 LSU game, Auburn, trailing 23–9, intercepted three straight LSU passes in the fourth quarter and returned all three for touchdowns in a 30–26 victory.

Not all of the unusual plays have gone Auburn's way.

- A "huddle" was used for the first time in the second half of the 1906 Georgia game. Having never seen a huddle, Auburn didn't know how to line up, and Georgia dominated the game from that point on, winning 12–6. The new huddle formation was one of several trick plays the Georgia coach, the legendary "Pop" Warner, considered by many to be one of the fathers of modern-day football, utilized that day in an effort to beat nemeses John Heisman and Auburn. Others included reverses and triple passes.
- In a controversial and highly disputed play, Georgia Tech finally got its first win over Auburn in 1906 after nine straight losses dating back to 1892, the first year of football at Auburn. The Georgia Tech punter, as planned, kicked the ball high in the air. A Tech player caught it and threw a pass to another Tech player for a touchdown. Georgia Tech 11–Auburn 0. Auburn, coached by Mike Donahue, argued mightily, but no rule was found against it, so the play stood. John Heisman, ever the trickster, was the Georgia Tech coach.

Then there was Blind Bill Turnbeaugh.

Lineman Bill Turnbeaugh, virtually blind, was one of the first players in the country to wear contact lenses in a game.

Contacts, new at the time, were big, bulky, and uncomfortable to wear under any circumstances. That one could wear them during a football game seemed impossible.

Because of his play in Auburn's surprising win over mighty Vanderbilt—no pun intended—Turnbeaugh received a lot of media attention. How, the media asked, can a virtual blind man see to play football?

Auburn sports publicist Bill Beckwith had the answer: "We call him 'hear-em, feel-em, grab 'em Turnbeaugh. He hears the play coming his way, he feels the pressure coming against him, and he just grabs everything coming his way until he gets the man with the ball, then he throws him to the ground."

Turnbeaugh resented that description the rest of his life. He considered himself a pretty good football player who never got the credit he deserved because of Beckwith's witty characterization, but the legend had been born.

And, as we all know from *The Man Who Shot Liberty Valance*, when the legend becomes fact, print the legend.

And it is legend, even unto this day.

One never knows what one might see at an Auburn football game.

It's been that way for 125 years. It will continue.

Held Captive

Went to a zoo, sort of, today and looked at the animals in their cages.

We humans have something in common with those caged animals. We, too, are caged—held captive by the bodies in which our souls and spirits reside.

One day, we—our spirit—will be free, free to soar to worlds unknown and unimaginable.

Until then, we are held captive by our bodies as the animals are held captive in their cages.

We are spiritual creations with a physical dimension, not physical creations with a spiritual dimension.

It is in the spirit that we live, breathe, and have our being.

Wisdom

The older I get, the more I appreciate the wisdom of children's literature.

There is often more truth in fable and parable than in fact.

This came to mind recently when a dear friend—a much beloved and respected friend—stepped down from a position he had held for almost forty years, relinquishing control of a corporation he had nurtured to life and prosperity. It was one of the constants in his life and in the life of the community where he lived.

His retirement request accepted, changing of the guard ratified, sentimentality was about to become the order of the day.

Then, of all times, at of all places, Dr. Seuss's wisdom came to mind: "Don't cry because it's ending, smile because it happened."

Any tinge of sadness and regret quickly turned to affirmation, respect, and deep appreciation of all the good this good, wise, and capable man had done and will continue to do in his role as chairman emeritus. This good and great man's race is not yet run.

What could have been a moment of sadness turned into moments of joy and celebration. As it should have.

"Don't cry because it's ending, smile because it happened…"

Dr. Seuss was a wise man.

We would do well to listen. And to heed.

It All Began on a Front Porch

One seldom knows where the ties that bind begin. But for Pat Dye, it began on the front porch of his farm home near the tiny hamlet of Blythe, Georgia, in 1957. He and his brothers were doing something in the backyard—probably fighting, he later said—while their father, Frank Wayne Dye, visited with an old friend, Shug Jordan, the football coach at Auburn.

Jordan, whose team would win the national championship later that year, spent most of his time sitting on the front porch, having a drink with Dye's father, catching up and swapping stories. Maybe even telling a few lies, as men are wont to do at times.

Right before he left, Jordan asked the elder Dye if he could speak to his youngest son, Pat. Frank Wayne called his son to the front porch.

Jordan didn't pressure Dye. Just the opposite. He had known the Dye family a long time, from his coaching days at Georgia, and he knew their situation as it related to football.

"Pat, we want you to come to Auburn," Jordan said. "I want you to know that, but I also know your brothers played at Georgia, and I can understand why you might think you ought to go to Georgia too.

"But I want you to know there will always be a place for you at Auburn."

There will always be a place for you at Auburn ...

Twenty-four years later, after an All-America playing career at Georgia and the start of a promising coaching career, Dye accepted another offer from Auburn, this time to become head football coach.

Auburn, Auburn football—and Auburn University—will never be the same. It will be forever better because he came. Because he came, and because he became an Auburn Man.

Jordan used to say that some people who become Auburn people by choice wind up loving Auburn and appreciating it more than some who grew up Auburn fans and went to school here. Pat Dye is such a man.

His record as head football coach, four SEC championships in seven years, the 1983 New York Times' National Championship, and the fact that the playing field at Jordan-Hare Stadium bears his name, Pat Dye Field, has been well chronicled and rightly so. But to limit Pat Dye's contribution to football alone would do a great injustice to him and to Auburn.

The man who would take Jordan's place as the face of Auburn football for the next generation left little doubt early on that he was committed to all of Auburn, not just Auburn football.

In his first year as athletics director and head football coach, Dye directed that all of the funds from Auburn's annual A-day spring game be divided evenly between the band, the A-Club, and the library.

Not long after that, he donated a million dollars of Athletics Department revenue to the library's capital fund drive.

"All the students use the library," he said. "That's why we want to support the library. It's important to the students, it's important to Auburn, and that makes it important to the Athletic Department."

That was the first of innumerable contributions to Auburn as a whole in terms of time and money.

Nearing the end of his life, Dye said, "If I live another eighty years, I could never repay Auburn for what Auburn has done for me." But he tried.

In retirement, wherever he was wanted, wherever he was needed, he would go, for the alumni association—he loved being with Auburn people; they energized him—to scholarship donor dinners, to fundraising events for virtually every academic unit within the university. Wherever he was wanted, wherever he was needed, wherever he could help, he would go.

He personally contributed to the Jule Collins Smith Art Museum, College of Veterinary Medicine, College of Agriculture, College of Architecture, Design, and Construction, Women's basketball, Enrollment Services, and the Harbert College of Business. Student scholarships were a primary area of emphasis in his giving. He continued to support Ralph Brown Draughon Library as he had since his first days at Auburn. It was important to the students; it was important to him.

His favorite cause, however, was the Blue Jean Ball held annually at his beloved Crooked Oaks farm to benefit the School of Nursing. He looked forward to that each year as he had once looked forward to the start of football season.

Pat Dye was not a perfect person, none of us are, but no one could ever question his love and commitment to Auburn.

As a friend said, "His passion for Auburn was contagious. It affected anyone and everyone no matter their race or situation in life."

He became the face not only of Auburn athletics but of Auburn itself. That teenager who visited with an Auburn legend on the front porch sixty-three years ago became an Auburn legend himself.

Jordan died in 1980, a year before Dye came to Auburn, but they joined hands across the ages, "down through the years," as Jordan would say, to make Auburn a better place to live, to learn, and to compete.

Together they touched the lives of Auburn men and women for more than seventy years, generations of Auburn people.

They made a difference.

Pat Dye, head football coach, athletics director.

But he was more, much, much more.

Pat Dye, Auburn Man.

That's all that need be said.

Pat Dye, Auburn Man.

Pat Dye

Truth from a Soap Opera

Wisdom from *General Hospital*'s Franco Baldwin: "The day will come when a person's life, all the good they've done, all the smiles and memories they've left, will not be overcome by memories of that person's death …"

Wise man, Franco Baldwin, wise man.

"The day will come when a person's life, all the good they've done, all the smiles and memories they have left, will not be overcome by memories of that person's death …"

The Past, Prologue to the Future

As we come to the end of this 125-year observance of Auburn football, the time has come to look ahead to the next twenty-five, fifty, and one hundred years.

As is written on the historical marker at Ross Square, site of Auburn's first football field, "Owing much to the past, Auburn's greater debt is ever to the future."

When I think of Auburn's past and Auburn's future, I think of Ed Dyas and Daniel Carlson.

Daniel Carlson never knew Ed Dyas, maybe never even heard of him.

But they have a lot in common.

Ed Dyas was a good person, a good student, and a good football player.

Daniel Carlson is a good person, a good student, and a good football player.

Daniel Carlson has become the most prolific kicker in SEC history. There was a time when that was true of Ed Dyas too.

In 1960, four of Auburn's eight wins came on field goals by Ed Dyas. He kicked an NCAA record thirteen field goals that year. He was an All-American and an Academic All-American.

He was the epitome of what an Auburn football player should be and what we, as fans, want our players to be.

As was Ed Dyas, so is Daniel Carlson.

Ed Dyas wore 38, and Daniel Carlson wears 38.

Every time Daniel Carlson goes on the field, I can't help but think about Ed Dyas. And when I think of Ed Dyas, my friend and one of my first football heroes, I think about Daniel Carlson.

It's not just the number 38 they share, it's the way they live their lives and the way they conduct themselves. The way they represent Auburn.

So many years apart, so much alike.

As Ed Dyas and his teammates paved the way for Daniel Carlson and his teammates, so Daniel Carlson and his teammates pave the way for those who will follow them.

Upon his retirement in 1975, Coach Shug Jordan established an annual award to go to the outstanding senior player each season.

Its inscription reads: "Down through the years outstanding Auburn football players have become outstanding citizens. Knowing this truth and having a deep and abiding faith in these men, I am proud to honor Auburn's outstanding senior football player with this award."

That is one of the things, one of the qualities and characteristics Auburn needs to carry into the next twenty-five, fifty, and one hundred years. I believe it will.

In looking ahead, we all want the same things everyone else wants: more wins, more championships, more national championships.

We all know that the game of football as it is played today will be vastly different in years to come. Mothers and lawyers will see to that.

When Bo Jackson says he might not have played football had he been aware of the concussion concerns of today, that alone should tell us that football will change. It has to change; it must change.

But twenty-five, fifty, and one hundred years from now, football will still be the most colorful, most popular sport on campus, but it may resemble soccer of today more than football of today. Football will still be a contact sport—it always will be—but the intensity of that contact will be greatly diminished.

But that is not a cause for sadness or concern. The football of today is nothing like the football played back in 1892 when George's Petrie's first Auburn team defeated Georgia, as Auburn did again three weeks ago.

Auburn's only play on that long ago day was something called the Flying Wedge. It resembled a rugby scrum more than what we call football today. The only thing certain in life is change.

Nobody knows what the future will hold, but we know this: there will be a place for Auburn in that future.

Someone once said the past is only prologue to the future.

Ed Dyas and Daniel Carlson are proof of that.

So on we go, to the next twenty-five, fifty, and one hundred years, knowing, believing, confident that our best days are still ahead. The best is yet to come.

And it may be just around the corner.

Owing much to the past, Auburn's greater debt is ever to the future.

The Color Purple

My Democratic friends think I am a Republican; my Republican friends think I am a Democrat.

My conservative friends think I am a liberal; my liberal friends think I am a conservative.

That's exactly where I want to be—an independent—free to vote for the best man or woman, free to vote for the best plan, position, or program, free to vote as I please, not bound by labels of red or blue.

Color me purple—a mixture of red and blue.

We need more purple in our politics today …

Another One Bites the Dust

It's a sad day today.

Another small, family-owned business has bit the dust, Flowersmith's Florists in what the locals call Downtown Auburn.

This is not a treatise on the state of the American economy or the difficulties small, family-owned businesses face. Nor is it a criticism of the new owner of the building where Flowersmith's has been located for fifty-six years, ever since 1961.

The new owner, whoever he or she may be, had every right to send word on December 1 that Flowersmith's had to vacate the building by December 31. That's the world of business today. The messenger who delivered the news said the new owner was, in his words, "all business." No problem with that. That's his or her right and, perhaps, responsibility.

But this is about none of that.

This is about Bobby and Sally Barrett and their daughter, Susan.

Bobby and Sally were two of the first people I met in Auburn back in 1965. They became fast friends, and many a Saturday morning were spent sitting in their small shop, drinking coffee and talking about all things Auburn, especially sports, football in particular. Bobby, who died in 2007, was one of the best Auburn men I've ever known, one of the best in every way.

It was especially fun at Christmas with all of the greenery, all of the poinsettias, all of the other beautiful flowers and the fragrances that came with them. It was the aroma of Christmas.

The coffee was always good, and so were the cookies and brownies Sally always seemed to have around that time of year.

Bobby, Sally, and later Susan knew their customers, knew them by name, knew their likes, dislikes, and the price range they were comfortable spending.

More than once, almost always, when sending flowers, I would call, tell Sally or Susan where to send the flowers, and close by saying, "Send 'em something nice."

It was always nice, just the right thing, at just the right time, at just the right price. They had that touch, that human touch, the touch of compassion, caring, and understanding.

They even had charge accounts back when charge accounts were in vogue. That was more than a little help to students making their way through Auburn on a sometimes tight budget. I don't know if they were always paid or not. I hope they were.

And now they are closing.

There are other places to buy flowers in Auburn, but Publix, Kroger, and Winn-Dixie can never replace the caring countenance of Bobby, Sally, and Susan.

And there are other small, family-owned florists in Auburn, good ones too, but there will always be something missing at 130 North College Street.

And there will always be a hole in my heart.

Flowersmith's will soon be gone.

Defining Moments

We just finished an outstanding video study of life's defining moments by Andy Stanley of Atlanta.

He defined death as life's eighth and most defining moment.

I disagree. How we face death, our attitude toward death and dying, is our most defining moment. Not death itself. We all die.

How do we face death? Do we fear it? Do we have trouble conceptualizing or conceiving of a world without us in it? Or do we grow to accept death as part of life, as Kathryn Tucker Windham said near the end of her life: "Death is life's next great adventure."

Shakespeare put it this way when he had Julius Caesar say, "It seems to me most strange that men should fear death since death, a necessary end, will come when it will come."

Death is not our defining moment. How we face death is our most defining moment.

For centuries, eons, ages, religion has held out the hope or assurance of a great beyond to make believers do what that religion says they should do.

But shouldn't there be more? Shouldn't we be told how to live, rather than how to die? Religion and faith owe us that much.

From a Christian perspective, far too many Christians spend far too much time thinking about and sometimes defending the virgin birth and the resurrection without giving much, if any, thought as to how Jesus lived between those two events, what he did and what he said we should do.

Start. Finish. For many Christians, that is the sum of their faith. Start, finish, nothing in between.

But there is more to being a Christian than a celestial fire insurance policy. The same holds true for other faiths.

We go to funerals and hear how great the dearly departed was, how nice, kind, and loving they were, how they were so important in our lives, how much good they did, and how much good they left behind. Sometimes it's true, sometimes not.

But when it is true, shouldn't we say those things when the person is living rather than wait until they are in a casket or their ashes in an urn?

A member of our class told of a reflective time shared with several other couples, all friends like family, friends who were family. It began in a humorous vein, joking about what the preacher would say about them when they made their inevitable final trip down the aisle. Then it turned personal.

"We began to pick one word to describe what that person meant to us," she said. "It was one of the most meaningful experiences of our lives. We all knew how we felt about each other, but this was the first time we had ever said it out loud. It meant so much to each of us to hear those words."

I have a friend who is ill. She doesn't know whether or not her illness will take her life. What she does know is that because of age and infirmity alone, she has a decreasing number of days to live.

And when that time comes, be it near or far, she wants her friends and loved ones to know how much they have meant to her. She goes out of her way to tell them, now, while she is living. "I want you to know I love you, and I am so grateful that you have been a part of my life. And I want you to remember that …"

The first time she said those words to me, I thought, or assumed, the end was near and that we would soon be gathering for what would be her final trip down the center aisle. "Oh, no," her husband said. "It's nothing like that. She just wants people to know she loves them and how much she appreciates them loving her."

Wouldn't the world be a better place if we all did that, expressed more love, expressed more care, more appreciation?

If we gave more hugs.

It's not death that defines us; it's how we live.

He Changed My Life

Gillis Morgan is dead.

He made me a better man.

Not by his long and distinguished journalism career or in his years of teaching journalism at Auburn.

He made me a better man by his criticism. And by coming to church.

Those were the days of the Auburn wars, everybody against somebody, somebody against everybody. The alumni association was against the board of trustees, and the board of trustees was against the alumni association. The faculty, the president, the students, all mixed in together, all fighting one another.

Nobody liked anybody; nobody trusted anybody. It was a mess, a morass really, a hard, trying time for Auburn and for anybody who loved and cared about Auburn.

Each of the many sides was determined to win the argument, the fight and the battle, even if it meant "burning the damn place down," a metaphor that was often used at the time.

The Athletics Department and I, as athletics director, were caught in the middle of it all, nowhere to turn, no good way out.

Gillis was a columnist for a local newspaper. He ripped me pretty good on occasion; sometimes I deserved it, sometimes not. But it did seem that he was beginning to enjoy the criticism a bit too much. Or so I thought. Or so I felt.

I would read all this stuff and then go to church to be an usher or a greeter. Every Sunday, just hours after reading his stinging criticism, Gillis and his wife, Gerry, would cross the street and head to the door where I was standing. He wasn't specifically seeking me out. I was standing at the main door. There was nowhere else to go.

It is easy enough to grit your teeth, smile, and say "Hey, how are you doing? Good to see you this morning. Hope you have a good day …"

In other words, lie.

As an usher, it was easy enough to get them through the door, down the aisle, into a seat, and then not have to see them anymore.

I hate to say this, and it's embarrassing to say this, but I may have been getting a tad self-righteous.

Then it all changed.

I was asked to help serve the Lord's Supper on Communion Sunday, usually the first Sunday of the month.

As Gillis walked down the aisle row by row and prepared

to kneel at the altar, I was overcome by a sea of conflicting emotions.

I can't do this, I thought. *I can't feel the way I feel and serve this man the Lord's Supper. This is His table; these are His elements, not mine. I can't do it.*

Then my eyes were opened. And I saw the light.

There was only one thing to do. I had to pray for him, for Gillis Morgan, my adversary. Not that he would come to see things my way but that he would have the same peace, fulfillment, and enrichment in his life that I wanted in mine. There was no other way.

There were others too, but Gillis provided the watershed moment. I would never be the same in any aspect of my life.

As M.L. Stedman wrote in her wonderful book *The Light Between Oceans,* "I choose to forgive. I can let myself rot in the past, spend my time hating people or I can forgive.

"You only have to forgive once. To resent, you have to do it all day, every day. You have to keep remembering all the bad things.

"We always have a choice, all of us."

Forgiveness does not come easily, and sometimes it is hard work, but it is the only way to go if you want to have a peaceful, fulfilled life, a life of joy and contentment.

I told Gillis about all of this one Friday morning after breakfast at Chappy's. He seemed stunned. "I didn't know."

But I knew.

I knew this man had changed my life.

Changed it forever.

Gillis Morgan

(1934–2018)

Rest in peace, my friend, rest in peace.

Words to Live By

Football is a terrific game, but a terrible god …

—Former Alabama player and Trinity High School football coach Randy Ragsdale at his induction into the Alabama High School Sports Hall of Fame

Running Naked through the Streets

Second Samuel—or Samuel 2, as Donald Trump might say—tells us that David, a man after God's own heart, once danced naked in the street. Just how naked depends on which version or translation of the Bible you read.

But David, King David, a man after God's own heart, ran naked or virtually naked through the streets.

Wonder why we never hear any sermons preached on that?

Alabama Politics

When I think about Alabama politics, I think about the last line of the movie *Bridge over the River Kwai:* "Madness, madness, sheer madness ..."

It is an apt comparison.

Start, Finish, Little or Nothing in Between

Far too many Christians spend far too much time thinking about and sometimes defending the virgin birth and the resurrection without giving much, if any, thought as to how Jesus lived between those two events, what he did, what he said we should do, what he said our values should be, and how those values—his values—should be evident in our daily lives.

Birth. Resurrection. Start. Finish. For too many Christians, that is the sum of their faith: virgin birth, resurrection, and nothing in between.

Say, "I accept Jesus Christ as my personal Lord and Savior," and you are set: an eternity walking on streets of gold within walls of jasper.

But there's more to being a Christian than a celestial fire insurance policy.

Saying "I accept Jesus Christ as my personal Lord and Savior" is not enough.

Remember what Jesus said: "I am the way, the truth, and the light …"

We don't need—we can't—forget that "way" part.

The hard part of loving Jesus comes in that word *way*.

Words come easy. Loving as Jesus said we should does not. Loving as Jesus said to love is hard, it is difficult, and sometimes it is uncomfortable.

But we are to love anyway. We can't forget, but we can forgive; we don't have to like people, but we do have to love people, people who are like us and people who are different from us. We are to love.

That is Jesus's way. And if we accept him, we have to accept his way.

If we say, "I take Jesus Christ as my personal Lord and Savior," but don't follow his way, our words, high sounding though they may be, are nothing but words, sounding brass or a tinkling cymbal …

That Thrilling Day of Yesteryear

Return with us now to that thrilling day of yesteryear, December 3, 1949.

The Alabama game never comes around that I don't think about that day. I was only three years old and have no recollection of it at all, but it has grown in legend and lore, as Coach Jordan would say, "down through the years ..."

Alabama had beaten Auburn—embarrassed Auburn—55–0 the year before in the first game played between the two schools in forty-one years.

The break was not caused by a big fight in which somebody died, as many thought for a long time. No, nothing like that. It was caused by something earthier than that: money.

For the 1908 game, Auburn wanted to take twenty-two players and pay $3.50 per diem. Alabama wanted to take twenty players and pay $3.00 per diem, a difference of about seventeen dollars a day or thirty-four dollars for the entire trip.

As is so often the case, pride and ego got involved. Next

there was a disagreement on a date for the game, then a disagreement on officials. Both sides became entrenched, and, as a result, there was no Auburn-Alabama game for forty years.

But back to December 3, 1949. Auburn was bad, really bad, with a record of 1–4–3, going into the game. Alabama was 6–2–1 and, again, a heavy favorite.

Still basking in the glow of the previous year's 55–0 victory, Alabama fans were flush with confidence.

As the Auburn players were getting on busses at their hotel for the short ride to Legion Field, some Alabama fans, perhaps inebriated, perhaps supremely confident, waved fifty- and hundred-dollar bills at the Auburn players, taunting that Alabama would score fifty-six that day.

Max Autrey and Travis Tidwell, who told this story forty-three years later, put this in their hearts and pondered it as they drove down Eighth Avenue toward the stadium. Forty-three years later, they still remembered.

Auburn scored first when Johnny Wallis intercepted a pass and returned it eighteen yards for a touchdown. Alabama tied the game 7–7 just before the half, but it was already a moral victory for Auburn. There would be no "fifty-six" this year. Not today.

Using the great Travis Tidwell as a decoy, Auburn drove seventy-one yards for a touchdown early in the fourth quarter. Now, if Auburn could just hold 'em. Auburn couldn't.

Alabama drove fifty-one yards in the closing minutes of the game and lined up for what appeared to be the tying extra point. Appeared to be. That's the operative term. *Appeared to be.*

Tidwell took credit for what happened next. He had played high school football against the Alabama kicker Eddie Salem, and Salem, Tidwell said, "knew about my speed and quickness."

"Line me up on the outside, and I can block it," he told Coach Earl Brown.

Tidwell didn't block it, but Salem missed it.

"He saw me come into the game," Tidwell said forty-three years later. "Right before the ball was snapped, he looked over to see where I was. That broke his concentration, and he missed the kick."

Auburn ran out the clock and had one of its sweetest victories ever, 14–13.

Auburn fans didn't want to leave the stadium. They stayed and stayed, celebrated and celebrated, ripping apart the feather-filled seat cushions that were rented at the game.

They left only when night came. The west stands and much of the field were covered with feathers. It was said to be the last time feather cushions were ever used at Legion Field.

The party continued long into the night, especially at the Thomas Jefferson Hotel, headquarters for Auburn alumni, fans, and students. Amid the revelry, an Auburn student,

Stringbean Jennings, fueled by victory and perhaps a bit of alcohol, made his way to the end of the hall and placed a collect call to the queen of England.

When informed the queen was sleeping and did not wish to be disturbed, Stringbean didn't miss a beat. "Well, when Her Majesty wakes up, you tell her Auburn just beat the hell out of Alabama, 14–13."

No one knows what will happen in this year's game—we hope we know, but we really don't.

But, just in case you need it, the international area code for London and Buckingham Palace is 020.

Good Advice

"I choose to believe the truth, no matter how I feel ..."
Good advice today.
Good advice every day.
"I choose to believe the truth, no matter how I feel ...

Sad State of Affairs

It's sad. It really is.

Every candidate running in the Alabama Republican primary, including the coroner, is trying to out-Trump Trump and out-Jesus Jesus.

Sad.

Trump probably loves it. Jesus, I dare say, is saddened, maybe even embarrassed by it all. Every candidate talks about his or her Christian values. Christian values are good, but they are far more meaningful when lived out in one's life rather than talked about at election time.

Shouldn't our politicians offer us something more?

New ideas? New plans? New suggestions on how to make our state and the lives of its people better? Don't the people of Alabama deserve at least that much?

Alabama may be forty-ninth or fiftieth in everything else, but when it comes to loving Trump and Jesus—at least saying we love Jesus—Alabama is faraway number one.

But shouldn't there be more?

A Divided Fourth

We approach our annual Fourth of July celebration a divided nation, probably as divided as we have been in our lifetime, though the Vietnam era was close.

We can't agree on much of anything, and we demonize the people who disagree with us as liberals, conservatives, intolerables, and who knows what else.

We have lost our common ground, that sacred place where we, as fellow Americans, could come and discuss our ideas and opinions with respect and reason and without fear of reprisal, whether that reprisal be words, fists, or something worse.

That's what this day is all about—or is supposed to be about. That's what this country is supposed to be about.

We blame Congress, the political parties, and sometimes the media for all our problems.

But they aren't the problem. We are the problem.

We are the problem because we cannot reasonably and respectfully discuss the issues of the day in the streets, villages, hamlets, and neighborhoods where we live without rancor and the use of labels to demean those who have a different view from ours.

Our political discussion has become like trench warfare in World War I. Nobody wins; everybody loses, most of all the country we profess to love.

I take great comfort in President George W. Bush's observation: "Sometimes the ship of state veers left, sometimes it veers right, but it always comes back toward the center and moves forward."

There is hope, and there is an example to follow. We of this generation say that the presidential election of 2016 was the most divisive in our history. Maybe it was, maybe it wasn't.

The election of 1800 pitted Thomas Jefferson and John Adams, two of the founding fathers, against each other.

It was dirty, vile, and bitter, just as the election of 2016 was. The issues were much the same: the role of government in our lives, the future of the country, and how we best get to that future.

As always, the personalities of the two men running played a major part as well. These two great founding fathers were bitter enemies, personal as well as political and professional.

There was no respect to be had. There was no Commons, no middle ground.

Yet, near the end of their lives, they became friends, best of friends, friends that were closer than brothers, and they worked together for the good of the country they both so strongly loved.

And that brings us back to the matter of the Fourth of July.

Can we, for one day, put down our weapons and check our rhetoric at the door?

Can we, for one day, for just one day, celebrate the way John Adams said we should celebrate? "With pomp and parades, with shows, games, sports, guns, bells, bonfires and illuminations from one end of the continent to the other …"

Thomas Jefferson, as much as he hated Adams at the time, would have wholeheartedly agreed.

We need to heed Adams's and Jefferson's example.

They have shown us the way once before, and they could show us the way again if we would only stop, look, listen … and learn.

The Fourth of July. A chance once again to remember and to become all that we could be and should be, as people and as a nation.

We can start by listening to one another rather than screaming at one another.

Lessons Learned in the Hospital

Lessons learned from six weeks in the hospital. In my case, EAMC, East Alabama Medical Center in Opelika.

The nurses were kind and professional as they provided services that only registered nurses could perform. But the real heroines of the hospital are the nursing techs, the patient care assistants, PCAs. They provide the tenderness and care that helps, maybe even enables, you to make it through.

When you are bedridden for several days and can't take care of your basic needs, all sense of pride and dignity goes away. But the techs, the patient care assistants, are there, meeting those needs with patience and understanding.

Many of the patient care assistants were women of faith, and you could sense it in the kind, gentle, tender, and caring way in which they worked and went about meeting your every need.

More than once, I thought about Jesus washing the feet of his disciples. The techs, the patient caregivers, did the same thing for me. I shall never forget them, and my gratitude is enduring.

They are paid for what they do, but they could never be paid what they are worth.

Doubt and fear came in the morning, in the wee small hours before daylight. Darkness is an appropriate metaphor. *Will I be able to do this? What if I'm bedridden forever, in a wheelchair, a nursing home?*

Fear is a dangerous thing, but thank goodness it was, in my case, a temporary thing. Fear is the opposite of faith, and joy still cometh in the morning. With the sunrise, with light, came hope.

When the physical therapists came in, they brought new hope. The fear, depression, and anxiety of the night turned into expectation and anticipation of the good that was going to come out of that morning's work.

Good therapists are like good coaches. They push you, cajole you, challenge you, encourage you, and praise you but only when it is deserved and earned. One of my therapists even used Auburn football examples to challenge and spur me on. He knew me well.

More than once, I thought of the truisms of my youth, especially *The Little Engine That Could*. Laugh and smile if you will, but there is great truth in that little tale. "I think I can, I think I can, I think I can … I thought I could, I thought I could, I thought I could …" Those words and that story came to mind again and again as I tried to work my way up the little incline in the skilled nursing facility.

I made it up that incline again and again, finally with ease. And when I was asked, I flexed those knees just a little more each time, a little farther than I thought I could go, all because someone in my youth or childhood told me a story about a little train engine that thought he could.

And the lessons from my old high school football coaches, Tommy White and Pete Steele, "Do what you are asked to do, then do it one more time." "One more time, one more time," I heard those words over and over in my mind, and I did whatever was asked one more time. Every time.

It was probably a much slower start for me than for most double-knee-replacement patients, but I made it through. Up and about again, doing my rehab every day in the hope, expectation, and anticipation of getting better, of being my old self again. Or even better.

I have come to a new appreciation of the tortoise and the hare. I may be a tortoise, but I am going to be a winner. Just you wait and see.

We often say we will keep someone in our thoughts and prayers when they are going through hard times. Some of us do; most of us don't. Many people told me they would keep me in their thoughts and prayers, and I know they did. I felt them, felt uplifted and empowered by them. Those thought and prayers helped me make it through. To all who lifted me up, I say, "Thank you." But that doesn't seem like enough. Far from it.

But the most important thing I learned from my forty-four-day stay in the hospital was simply this:

I have spent a lot of time talking about God over the years.

I need to spend more time talking to God.

All Good Things Must Come to an End

A record of sorts will end today.

A personal record.

I will miss my first Auburn home game in fifty-three years.

Not since the Georgia game of 1964, the last game of that season, have the Tigers played in Auburn without me being there to cheer them on, to live and die with them.

I missed that Georgia game because I was at Livingston State College, now the University of West Alabama, taking the ACT test so I could come to Auburn.

Recovering from double-knee-replacement surgery, I am not sure how many home games I will miss this year. It matters little. I have a big-screen TV and memories. Oh, the memories.

I have not counted the games in the streak, the record, points scored, or anything like that. On this Saturday morning before the streak ends, only the memories matter.

From that first one as a freshman in in 1965, an upset loss to Baylor, to the last one, the 26–14 win over Alabama last year, it's been a joyful, sometimes tempestuous ride, but it's always been worth the investment of hopes, dreams, and fears that accompany following any college football team and, of course, the agony or ecstasy that follows.

I've seen Cliff Hare Stadium become Jordan-Hare Stadium, seen it grow from 44,000 seats in 1965 to more than 87,000 in 2018. I've outlived two press boxes, one of which bears my name. The biggest win, the best, the most exciting, the most disappointing? They all run together after a while. Almost.

Except the biggest, most memorable games, 30–20, Kick Six, the Prayer in Jordan-Hare, and the Interception Game against LSU in 1994.

There were others too, perhaps memorable only to me but memorable just the same.

The 31–7 upset win over highly ranked Miami on Homecoming in 1968, the 28–17 win over Steve Spurrier and the Florida Gators in 1965, Bill Cody's great day.

Scott Etheridge's field goal to beat Florida in 1993 and keep the unlikely dream alive. The 11-Oh-Oh-Oh season of 1993, Terry Bowden's first year, the Impossible Dream come true.

There were others too, not so enjoyable, and a few you just want to forget. Or wish you could. The 3–0 loss to Southern

Mississippi in 1965, my freshman year. Things like that just weren't supposed to happen.

The 17–9 homecoming loss to LSU in the rain in 1970, the loss to Georgia that same year that knocked us out of the Sugar Bowl. Some, like the 1980 Tennessee game and the 2012 Texas A&M game, are so painful we simply choose to forget.

The coaches, Coach Jordan, Coach Barfield, Coach Dye, Terry Bowden, Tommy Tuberville, Gene Chizik, and now Gus Malzahn. The players, far too many to name, are all there, in my mind, in my heart, and in my memory.

Along the way, I have come to have more respect for and appreciation of our opponents. No more of the spite and hate that I'm embarrassed to say describe the attitudes of my early years. But it was there. Then. Not now. When I became a man, I put away childish things. And those were childish thoughts, childish things. Very childish.

All of these things come to mind today to form a meaningful collage of my life with Auburn football here in Auburn.

I look back at that long-ago day, November 14, 1964, when I last missed a home game. I got mad and frustrated on the way home from Livingston because Jimmy McDaniel, the driver, wouldn't let me listen to the Georgia game. He and his Alabama buddies, one of whom was Larry Blakeney, a future Auburn quarterback, wanted to listen to the Alabama-LSU game.

That was the last time I've had to fret or worry about that.

As a student, a newspaper man, an instructor, an employee, and as a fan, I've seen every home game since. Fifty-three years, fifty-three good years.

But now it ends.

Time for a new story to begin.

A new story and a new streak.

A Farewell to Pat Sullivan

This column appeared in *Auburn Football Illustrated*, Auburn's game-day program in November 2014, day of the Auburn-Samford game. It was thought to be Pat Sullivan's last trip to Auburn in a football capacity. It proved to be true. Pat retired ten days later. This is one of the ways Auburn said goodbye.

One never knows, but it would appear, given his age—65 in January—and the fact that Samford does not appear on any future Auburn schedules, that this is likely Pat Sullivan's last trip to Auburn—his last trip home—in an official football capacity.

From this point on he will return in the same way he left: a hero. A hero who represents all that is good and noble about Auburn and Auburn Football. The name *"Pat Sullivan"* will symbolize and define the word *"hero"* in the tradition, legend and lore of Auburn Football forevermore. Forevermore.

When Pat Sullivan signed with Auburn in December of 1967, he gave Auburn people the same thing Bo Jackson would give them 14 years later: hope. Hope is the greatest thing an individual can give a nation or a people. Hope—the expectation, the assurance—of better things to come and the leadership and ability to make those dreams come true, to make things better.

Pat Sullivan delivered on that hope. He made those Auburn hopes and dreams come true. Never was the future more evident than in the freshman game—back when freshmen games were played—against Alabama at Tuscaloosa in 1968.

The highly touted Auburn freshman class fell behind Alabama 27–0 in the second quarter. It was embarrassing and could have been demoralizing. It could have been, that is, until Pat Sullivan stepped into the huddle when Auburn took the field after Alabama's 27th point.

He looked at each of his teammates in the huddle—looked each of them in the eye—and said, "We're going that way (toward the Alabama goal) and we're gonna win." And win they did, 36–27, in one of the all-time epic comebacks in Auburn Football history.

Back in Auburn, the varsity was going through a light practice in preparation for its game against Alabama the next weekend. Coach Shug Jordan was listening to the game on the radio and as the Sullivan-led Tiger Cubs began their comeback, he called off practice and told his players to gather around and listen with him. He knew a new day was dawning in Auburn Football, a new era was about to begin, and he wanted his players to gather with him and listen to what their future leader could do.

Sullivan did not disappoint, then or in the years to come. That was the first of three straight come-from-behind victories over Alabama. In 1970, Pat's junior year, Auburn trailed Alabama 17–0 at the end of the first quarter but came back to win 33–28. It was one of the most exciting, electrifying games in Auburn history. Simply put, it was a game for the ages.

Charles Land, Sports Editor of *The Tuscaloosa News*, wrote the next day *"Pat Sullivan may not be able to part the Red Sea, but he certainly has a way with Crimson Tides..."*

Pat would lead Auburn to 26 victories in three years at a time when teams played only 10 regular season games. His teams beat Alabama three out of four times, counting the freshman game, Florida and Georgia Tech three times, won two out of three from Tennessee and Georgia, and led Auburn to three bowls, including its first ever trip to the Sugar Bowl.

Those who were alive and care about Auburn Football will never forget the 1971 Georgia game in Athens. No SEC teams had met that late in the season undefeated. The railroad tracks were filled, as usual, and there were, literally, people in trees and on rooftops. In that intense, emotionally charged atmosphere, Sullivan had one of his best days as a Tiger leading Auburn to a 35–20 victory.

Venerable Georgia Coach Vince Dooley said it was the greatest performance by a quarterback he ever saw. Many say Pat won the Heisman Trophy that day with his play against undefeated Georgia.

How did Auburn people feel about Pat Sullivan's ability as a leader and as a football player? Jack Doane of the *Montgomery Advertiser* may have said it best on Sunday after Sullivan led an 86-yard game-winning late fourth quarter drive to beat Tennessee 10–9 in Knoxville in 1971. Jack wrote, *"Blindfolded, hands tied behind his back, Pat Sullivan would be a one-point favorite at this own execution."*

On the day his number "7" was retired, Pat stood next to the fence for hours signing every program and scrap of paper his adoring fans, most of them teenagers and little boys, put before him. This weekend as he makes what may be his last trip to Jordan-Hare Stadium in a football capacity, hundreds of those programs and little scraps of paper will be carefully brought forth from a myriad of Auburn treasure chests as fathers and grandfathers share once again the legend of Pat Sullivan with their sons and grandsons.

It is as it should be.

It is as it always will be.

Pat Sullivan, #7

Decline of the Methodist Church

Is it just me or has the Methodist Church been going downhill since it quit using the Cokesbury Hymnal?

Ellsworth Steele

Good man. Perhaps a great man.

He taught and provided leadership in the Economics Department and the College of Business for thirty-three years before retiring in 1982. He was a scholar and an intellectual. He was an Auburn treasure. Where his influence will end, we will never know.

Do we ever know where our influence will end? I think not, certainly for teachers and leaders like Ellsworth who put their students first. Always.

But that's not what I will remember when I think about Ellsworth in the years to come. I will remember something he did forty or more years ago in the early to midseventies at a called meeting of the administrative board of the Auburn United Methodist Church. He stood tall.

It was a called meeting of the board to consider whether or not the church should oppose a beer license for Pasquale's Pizza, which was located across the street from Friendship Hall, at the time the church's youth facility.

The discussion was passionate and heated. One argument

had to do with the number of beer cans that would surely be strewn across church property after a Saturday night of students drinking beer and eating pizza at Pasquale's. To have all those beer cans on the church lawn on Sunday morning would be a bad reflection on the church.

Another argument had to do with the evils of drinking beer and how it would lead to a life of alcoholism and debauchery.

Others said the church should not get involved. Pasquale's was located on private property, and the church had no right to say what should or should be done on private property.

The board was evenly divided. One vote ended in a dead-even tie. And nobody on either side seemed ready to budge.

If you've ever been involved in a good church fight, you know what I mean.

God had spoken to both sides, but he had, apparently, told each side different things.

Emotions were high and about to spill over when Ellsworth stood.

"I've only got one question," he said.

"How many of us had a beer or a drink before coming to this meeting? And how many of us are going to have a drink when we get home tonight?"

The room was quiet, and shortly thereafter, the board voted not to oppose the beer license. Hypocrisy avoided.

Ellsworth Steele, a good man?

No.

He was a wise and great man.

And he will be missed.

Missing

I've thought of her often over the years.

Especially at this time of the year.

That last line on the Christmas card list:

"Mrs. Thornell (Lost, 1993)"

What is it? Twenty-five years now since we've been in touch? That's a long time, but I'll never forget her. How could I?

Through her tender love and care, we were able to keep Momma at home during her last days. To the end. Mrs. Thornell and I were by her bedside when she took her last breath.

You don't forget things like that. Never.

Mrs. Thornell took care of Momma's every need, needs Momma didn't even know she had. I have previously written about patient care assistants in the hospital, those angels unaware who enable you to carry on when you've been there for extended periods of time. Mrs. Thornell was Momma's angel, her home caregiver, taking care of her when she was incapable of taking care of herself.

It takes a special person to do that. It's a special calling from God, and one has to have special gifts, gifts given only by God. Ms. Thornell had those gifts in rare degree.

I've thought about her often in the thirty years since Momma died. We stayed in touch for a while, usually at Christmas. Then came 1993, the returned Christmas card with the notation: *"Unable to deliver. No forwarding address."*

Mrs. Thornell. Lost. Gone.

I tried to find her over the years, always to no avail, and I eventually gave up trying.

Then late one night not long ago, while surfing a list of my Facebook "friends" (yes, I do that, as most of us do), I ran across the name "Thornell."

No, it couldn't be, I thought, but it was worth the try. An IM—an instant private message to you non-Facebook users—soon followed.

"Would you happen by chance to know a woman named Mrs. Lorena Thornell who cared for Estelle Housel in Gordo in the late eighties?" I asked.

To my surprise, minutes later came the response: "Yes, I'm her son."

The questions came quickly. Is she still living? How is she? Is she well? How can I get in touch with her?

He told me she was in a nursing home in a small town not far from where I grew up and where her son still lives.

Then came the hard but inevitable question, "Does she still have her mind?" or words to that effect.

No, he said. Dementia and age had taken their toll.

After all these years, I would not get to tell her what I so wanted to tell her. I would not get to thank her again, one more time.

So I did the only thing I could do. I told her son.

"I have thought about your mother so often over the years. She was a good woman, a great woman, who was so kind, so gentle, so caring.

"I wish I could tell her how often I've thought about her and how often I've thanked God for her.

"Your mother was a great human being. Not everyone could do what she spent her life doing.

"She was a blessing …"

As fate would have it, I was never able to tell her.

But I was able to tell her son.

That will have to be enough.

Favorite Christmas

In what seems like a long time ago in a galaxy far, far away, my brother and I were talking about our favorite Christmas memories.

As young boys are wont to do, our discussion centered on gifts received from Santa and others.

Daddy was sitting in his chair in the den listening. Occasionally he would tap his pipe in the ashtray (these were the days when everyone had ashtrays in their home), but he said nothing. He just listened.

My brother or I, one of us, asked Daddy about his favorite Christmas memory.

He said something nondescript like, "They're all my favorites," and tapped his pipe again.

Unwilling to let him off that easily, we insisted. "No, Daddy, tell us about your very favorite Christmas memory."

He tapped his pipe again, a bit harder this time, and said, "Well, if you really want to know, it was Christmas Day, 1944. The sky was black with bombers …"

Not expecting an answer like that, we pressed on for more. It was the only time he ever talked about his war experiences.

Here's the story:

It was Christmas Day, 1944, the Battle of the Bulge.

Hitler's seemingly defeated German army had mounted one last great offensive in a last-ditch effort to win the war. Hitler himself planned the attack. The goal was to reach the port of Antwerp on the Belgium coast, cutting Allied supply lines and splitting the Allied forces in two groups.

The Germans then planned to encircle and destroy four Allied armies, effectively ending the war on the western front, enabling them to concentrate their entire war effort on the hated Russians to the east.

Led by deadly Panzer and Tiger tanks, thirty German divisions attacked through the Ardennes, a broad, heavily forested area in eastern Belgium. The Allies had air superiority, but terrible weather conditions, including heavy fog, ice, and driving snow, kept aircraft grounded. There would be no air support in these conditions.

The speed of the German advance disrupted ground communications. Nobody had any real sense of where the Germans were or where they were going. Surprised American commanders knew a major battle was underway, their lines had been overrun, and troops were in dangerous disarray. They knew that and nothing more.

Daddy was with the Seventh Armored Division. His squad

had been surrounded in the heavy fighting around St. Vith. He found a way to lead them to safety and was later awarded the Bronze Star.

With the Germans advancing and the Americans in chaotic retreat, it seemed for a while that the Germans might reach their goal and alter the course of the war.

But as Christmas Day approached, General George S. Patton, old "Blood and Guts Patton," ordered his chaplain to write him a prayer for good weather. "You write me a good prayer," Patton supposedly said, "and I'll make sure it gets through."

Apparently, he was a man of his word.

Christmas Day dawned icy cold but bright and clear. And, as Daddy said, "the sky was black with bombers." Allied bombers. That's the reason Christmas, 1944 was his most memorable Christmas. It probably remained that way until the day he died, August 30, 1990, but he never talked about it again.

With air support, the Allies regained control of the battle and the war. Within five months, it was over, and the man who would become my father resumed the life he had known before, a sales clerk in the small-town, family-owned hardware business. In later years, two sons would be added to that life.

I, of course, was not alive in 1944, but after hearing Daddy talk about that Christmas, it became one of my favorite Christmases too.

It still is.

And I will never look at the term "favorite Christmas" the same way again.

Dave Housel

Cody Parkey

Saw something recently that I thought I would never see. Cody Parkey of the Chicago Bears lifted his index finger toward the heavens after missing what would have been the game-winning field goal with seconds left in the Bears' NFL playoff game against the Philadelphia Eagles.

It is rather common, perhaps a bit too common, to see quarterbacks, receivers, runners, kickers, and homerun hitters lift their finger toward the heavens as if to thank God for their moment of success.

It is easy to lift that finger toward heaven in moments of triumph and joy. Not so easy in times of misery and defeat, as Cody Parkey did at the end of the Bears game.

It is easy to thank God for our many blessings in good times, times of joy and plenty. Not so easy to thank God for those same blessings in times of disappointment, anguish, and defeat.

But that's what Cody Parkey did. It was the most powerful testimony of faith I have ever seen from an athlete.

There is a powerful lesson there for all of us who claim to share that same faith.

Neil Davis—A Hero for His Time

When I think of Neil Davis, one image comes to mind. In was in the sixties, and George Wallace, at the peak of his power, was standing on a flatbed trailer at Toomer's Corner, ranting and raving against the things he normally ranted and raved against, among them "them lying newspapers and their editors who won't stand with you and me as we 'Stand Up for Alabama.'"

His adoring throng of devotees, of which there were many, crowded in front of the trailer and cheered mightily as he told them they had one of those newspapers and editors right here in Auburn, the *Lee County Bulletin* and its editor Neil Davis.

"They don't want us to stand up for Alabama and our values," he said, "and until they do, you good people of Auburn and Lee County ought not to read that paper, ought not to subscribe to that paper and ought not to support its advertisers." Words to that effect.

Off to the side, just on the edge of the crowd stood Neil

Davis, faithfully making notes, taking down every word Wallace said, every insult, every challenge, every threat, every innuendo. The expression on his face never changed.

Neil Davis stood there like sentinel, a sentinel to all that was good and true, to all that was compassionate and caring to his fellow man, regardless of race, a pillar of strength against the venom, racism, and poison Wallace was espousing.

He went back to his office on Tichenor Avenue and wrote a fair and objective story on what Wallace said at Toomer's Corner.

Then, on the editorial page, he excoriated Wallace, his demagoguery, and all he proclaimed to stand for.

The *Lee County Bulletin* (and Neil Davis), he wrote, would not yield to threats and intimidation. If it lost subscribers and all or most of its advertisers, it would continue to speak out for fair and equal treatment for all citizens, especially those who were poor, downtrodden, disenfranchised, and had no one to speak for them.

It was not a popular stand to take, even in Auburn at that time, but it didn't matter. There was right, and there was wrong, and as far as Neil Davis and his paper were concerned, they were going to stand on the side of right, fairness, opportunity, and equality.

He became my hero that day.

Generations of Auburn citizens were strengthened and fortified over the years by his willingness to speak his opinion on a number of issues and back them up. Courage, integrity, and compassion were hallmarks of his character and his career as an editor and newspaper man.

His affect and influence spread far and wide.

To generations of Auburn journalism students, it wasn't so much WWJD but WWNDD.

What would Neil Davis do?

I am one of them, and I am a stronger, better person because Neil Davis came into my life.

He will posthumously receive the Auburn Alumni Association's Lifetime Achievement Award later this spring. It is the highest award the alumni association gives.

No man could deserve it more.

Neil Davis was a hero, for his time, and for mine.

Class Act

Eight years ago today, July 9, 2011, Derek Jeter got his three thousandth career hit, a line drive homerun over the left centerfield fence in Yankee Stadium.

I had the good fortune of being there, but it is not the homerun that I remember.

It's what happened after the homerun.

What I best remember—and what continues to have abiding meaning—is what happened after the crowd's long, loving roar of adulation, after the Tampa Bay Rays left their dugout and stood applauding as one as Jeter rounded third and headed home, after the tumultuous reception at home plate when Jeter hugged and embraced every one of his Yankees teammates and coaches.

After all of that.

What I remember most, and what continues to be one of the most memorable moments in my experience with sport, took place as Jeter made his way toward the Yankees dugout.

It was in that moment when the Rays pitcher, David Price, who had just given up the homerun, the three thousandth hit, got Jeter's attention and slowly, ever so slowly, ever so respectfully, tipped his cap.

It is that tip of the cap that will forever have meaning to me, a competitor's salute to an outstanding player for an outstanding accomplishment.

That tip of the cap.

You see more of that kind of thing in baseball than in any other sport.

And that is to baseball's credit.

One Hundred Days

So it is one hundred days until the first football game. Don't wish your life away, wanting, wishing, and waiting for football season to start.

At the end of your life, you will want these one hundred days back, all of them and more.

For everything, there is a season.

From Generation unto Generation

So, Auburn has named a starting quarterback, and it's Bo Nix, son of legendary Auburn quarterback Patrick Nix.

Auburn fans, of which I am one, can only hope his career equals or surpasses that of his father. And Patrick wants that too. Every father wants his son to be better than he was, and Patrick is no exception.

Patrick Nix burst on the Auburn football scene with one of the most memorable plays in Auburn history.

In 1993, with Auburn trailing Alabama 14–5 in the third quarter, Patrick Nix replaced injured quarterback Stan White and, without so much as throwing a single warmup pass, threw a thirty-five-yard touchdown pass to Frank Sanders on fourth and fifteen from the Alabama thirty-five. Without so much as a single warm-up toss.

The pass didn't win the game—Alabama still led 14–12—but the tone and focus of the game had changed. The hunter had become the hunted.

With the elder Nix at quarterback, Auburn became the aggressor and won 22–14 to cap off a highly improbable and unexpected season, the "11 and Ohhhhh" season.

Years later, in one of those Auburn football family reunion videos, Patrick, who grew up an Auburn fan, was asked about that play.

"People said I threw that pass without practicing. That's not true. I'd been practicing that pass all my life.

"It was the last pass I threw every day at practice or in the backyard before going in for supper. It was the always the last pass, the pass that beat Alabama. I'd been practicing that pass all my life."

Now his son finds himself in much the same situation.

All of his life, Bo Nix has dreamed of being the quarterback at Auburn. All of his life, as his daddy did before him, he has dreamed of making the big play to beat Alabama, Georgia, and other major rivals, dreamed of leading Auburn from victory unto victory. All of his life.

His time has come.

I, for one, can't help pulling for him.

Auburn football's past, present and future meet as Bo Nix greets Coach Pat Dye who recruited his father Patrick Nix to Auburn in 1991.

Freshman Bo Nix scores Auburn's first touchdown in a 48–45 victory over Alabama, November 30, 2019.

A Matter of Utmost Importance

Which is more important to your faith?
The birth or the resurrection?

Auburn-Georgia— Still the Best

The 1960 Georgia game may be, arguably of course, the most important game in Auburn history.

Not for who won the game, Auburn did 9–6, but for where the game was played—Auburn.

It was the first step toward realization of a goal, a dream Auburn people had for more than 30 years, that of playing all of its big games in Auburn. Georgia was then, as it is now, Auburn's oldest and most traditional rivalry. Some say its most meaningful rivalry.

When Jeff Beard and Shug Jordan were athletes at Auburn in the late 1920's, Auburn had to play all of its big games, sometimes all of its games, on the road.

That changed in 1951 when Beard became the Athletic Director and Jordan, the line coach at Georgia, became the head football coach at Auburn. They worked together to provide Auburn with facilities big enough and good enough to host all of its home games on campus.

That became reality in 1960 when Georgia came to Auburn for the first time. Actually, it had begun to change in 1959 when Jordan first took his Tigers to Athens. Auburn lost 14–13 as Georgia won Wally Butts' last SEC championship, but the Auburn-Georgia rivalry—and Auburn football—had changed forever. Not by who won, but by where the games were played.

It is worthy of note that of all Auburn's major rivals at the time, Tennessee, Georgia Tech, Georgia and Alabama, only Georgia, time-honored and respected foe Georgia, came to Auburn without a fight. Alabama fought hardest of all, saying it would never come, but it did, in 1989. Only Georgia came freely and voluntarily, band playing, red and black banners flying, as if to say "We're here; let's play." That has not been forgotten by Auburn people.

There is a story of how the game was moved from Columbus where it had been played consistently for more than 40 years. It wasn't an easy move.

Both schools wanted to move the game to campus, and both schools later used moving the game to justify major stadium enlargements, but Wally Butts was apprehensive, maybe a little fearful, of even broaching the subject of moving the game from Columbus.

There were lots and lots of bigtime Georgia supporters in Columbus, well-heeled old Coca Cola moneyed people, who freely and generously supported the Bulldogs—as long as the Auburn game was played in Columbus. Butts, rightly so, was afraid of incurring their wrath.

Beard and Jordan told him not to worry. They would take the heat so Butts could tell his people that he didn't want to move the game, that he fought as hard as he could to keep the game in Columbus, but "it's them damn Auburn people … they won't listen … they're unreasonable … don't blame me; don't blame Georgia … blame them damn Auburn people …"

It worked.

Cooperation and respect have always been hallmarks of this otherwise intense rivalry. Part of it is the history of the rivalry and part of it is the mutual understanding and appreciation that comes from the cross-breeding of the two football coaching staffs that has taken place down through the years.

Many Auburn men have gone to Georgia and won fame and acclaim, and many Georgia men have come to Auburn and won fame and acclaim. Jordan, Joel Eaves, Erk Russell, Pat Dye and Vince Dooley are only five examples. There are many, many more.

The cross pollination of coaching staffs, not just head coaches, led my friend Claude Felton, senior associate athletics director at Georgia, and the best Georgia man I know, to speculate there was an underground railroad running from Athens to Auburn and from Auburn to Athens. Those fortunate enough to have coached at both places were "War Dogs" or "Bull Eagles," depending on where they were coaching at the time. War Dogs were at Auburn. Bull Eagles were at Georgia.

The Georgia game was always Coach Jordan's favorite. It gave him the opportunity to see old friends, to visit a stadium and a campus he cared about and respected, and to write another chapter in what he considered the South's greatest rivalry. Vince Dooley had similar feelings when he carried his Georgia teams to Auburn, another example of the respect, mutual appreciation, and sometimes even admiration that has always marked this rivalry.

After Auburn's victory in the pivotal 1960 game in Auburn, Jordan said, "If Auburn and Georgia keep playing exciting games like this, we'll have to raise ticket prices to $10." Tickets to that game were $5.

Looking at the price of tickets today—$140—it is clear that Auburn and Georgia have continued to play exciting games, many, many, many of them.

Jordan studied history at Auburn, and the history of the Auburn-Georgia game always intrigued him. "After all these years," he once said, "after all the mud, the blood and the beer, Auburn and Georgia are still about even. That's probably the way it should be …"

Back when I was working, Claude Felton and I would often talk about the Georgia game, or, if you prefer, the Auburn game.

We agreed that when Auburn plays Alabama and Georgia plays Georgia Tech, it's like in-laws fighting, but when Auburn and Georgia play, it's like brothers fighting.

May it ever be so.

—Auburn foreword to *The Deep South's Oldest Rivalry: Georgia vs. Auburn* by Doug Stutsman. Written by David Housel. Used with permission of the book author, Doug Stutsman

Of Hopes, Fears, and All the Years

One point to ponder on this Christmas Eve.

> One point and one point alone:
> The last two lines of the first verse of "O, Little Town of Bethlehem."
> In context:

> Above your deep and dreamless sleep
> the silent stars go by.

> Yet in thy dark streets shineth
> the everlasting light,

> The hopes and fears of all the years,
> are met in thee tonight."

That's strong stuff.

> The hopes and fears of all the years,
> Are met in thee tonight.

Ponder that for a while.

Role Model

From my dear friend Bill Hancock, executive director of the College Football Playoff: "Random, goofy thought on a snowy day: who would make the more fabulous role model, Atticus Finch or George Bailey?"

Good question, Bill, great question …

Atticus Finch or George Bailey?

What say ye?

Auburn-Kentucky—Something Biblical

There was something biblical about the end of the Auburn-Kentucky basketball game yesterday.

Not in who won or lost the game. God doesn't care about things like that. That's a human concern, not God's concern.

What was biblical, to me at least, is something that didn't happen. Nobody rushed the floor.

For some reason, known but to God, it reminded me of a Jesus story, the one about the men, high priests, scribes, and Pharisees, those guys, bringing the woman caught in adultery to Jesus, trying to trick him, to trap him, as they always seemed to want to do.

They wanted to know if Jesus would follow the law and stone her—many, tradition says, already had rocks in hand—or would he not follow the law. He had broken the law so many times before.

Jesus simply squatted down, began drawing in the dirt,

and offered this thought: "Let he who is without sin cast the first stone …"

You know the rest of the story. The men, high priests, scribes, Pharisees, and all the others stood there a while and then, one by one, walked away.

I have often wondered what it would be like to have been there, to see the first man drop his stone and walk away. I'd like to talk to that man.

What does all of this have to do with the Auburn-Kentucky basketball game? Simply this: if one student, just one or two students, had rushed the floor Saturday, hundreds would have followed. But no one did, and no one followed.

What made me think about all of this? I don't know, but something did, and that same something is causing me to share it with you today.

Letter to the Lone Ranger

The coronavirus has done one good thing. It has given us time to look back, to go through old stuff, old boxes of keepsakes, to look at them again, to determine anew what's worth keeping and what should be / could be thrown away.

Here's one of my keepers, a letter to Clayton Moore, the Lone Ranger, written in 1995 after I had just gotten his home address:

May 24, 1995

Dear Mr. Moore,

I don't know that I have ever taken greater pleasure in writing a letter than I do this one.

Allow me to explain.

Growing up you were my hero, and as I have grown older, I have come to understand and appreciate to an even greater degree the impact that you, the Lone Ranger, had on my life and values, values that I carry with me even until this day.

When I was growing up, you, as the Lone Ranger, served as a role model, someone who stood for right, truth and justice. If you had the courage to stand for those qualities and principles, then you would be alright in the end.

I believed in that world then, and I believe in that world now.

Maybe a little childish perhaps, maybe a little naïve, but I still believe.

The sad part is that kids today don't get that message in their role models and TV heroes. They don't have Clayton Moore, and they don't have the Lone Ranger. That's too bad.

I'm glad that you and the Lone Ranger were there for me and for others of my generation in our formative years.

My travels occasionally take me to California, and I would welcome to opportunity to shake your hand and to tell you in person how much I appreciate the impact you and the Lone Ranger have had on my life.

In the event that meeting never occurs, I at least know that I have the pleasure of thanking you—and the Lone Ranger—for that influence.

Sincerely,
David Housel
Athletics Director
Auburn University

The Lone Ranger, because of age and infirmity, never responded. There was a telephone conversation a year or so later, and Clayton Moore, the Lone Ranger, continued to get a birthday card from Auburn, Alabama, each September 14 until he died in 1999.

The Lone Ranger

Gramma's Front Porch

The coronavirus has done one good thing. It has given us time to look back, to go through old stuff, old boxes of keepsakes, to look at them again to determine anew what's worth keeping and what should be/could be thrown away. Here is one of my keepers.

From the *Auburn Bulletin,* November 1973:

> When I was a kid I had this thing about Auburn football. No matter how well the Tigers blocked and tackled, they couldn't win unless I was in my lucky spot.
>
> And my lucky spot, more often than not, was on Gramma's front porch.
>
> There, through driving rain and freezing cold, I did my part to urge the Tigers on. If Tennessee beat them, or Tech, or Georgia, I had to change my lucky spot. If they didn't win, it was partially my fault, I was doing something wrong.

One time I would sit on the front porch, the next time in a chair, the next in the swing. Finally, in 20-degree weather, out of desperation, I moved to the sidewalk. It didn't do any good. Alabama won, 10–0.

Gramma could never understand her grandson. It was probably because she didn't understand football. She may have seen a game or two early in life, when her sons were playing, but she never saw a grandson play.

"Afraid they might get hurt," she would say. That was another of saying arthritis or rheumatism.

But you know grandmothers. Whatever pleases grandchildren pleases them, so she was more than happy to have me interrupt her Saturday afternoons on behalf of Auburn football.

Unless you are a grandmother, you don't know what it means. It means no piano playing, no phone calls, no visitors, nothing to detract from the seriousness of the game. She tried to sleep once, but had to give up after Jimmy Pettus ran the opening kickoff all the way against Kentucky.

So, while my outlook on life was being determined at Cliff Hare Stadium, Gramma would sit quietly in her living room and sew or read the Bible.

On certain lucky Saturdays, she would ease my pain or increase my joy with a slice of orange cake. Only Gramma could make a cake like that.

That was part of growing up with Auburn football in a town so remote that only one or two trips a year were possible.

Gramma never understood it. At best she tolerated it. She was glad when Auburn won and sad when Auburn lost—not so much for Auburn but for her grandson—whose world had just fallen apart.

I wish I could go back. Go back just one more time. Hug her, kiss her and tell her that she really was the World's Greatest Grandma. I wish I could, but I can't.

She fell the other day, broke her hip and separated a shoulder. Her chances of coming back aren't too good. She's 95. That's pretty far along in the fourth quarter of life to be staging a comeback.

When Auburn and Mississippi State kickoff Saturday, I'll think about Gramma.

Winning and losing won't seem so important.

I'll think about Gramma's front porch, the good times—and the bad. Those are the real Saturdays to remember.

Gramma

April 8, 1974

The night Henry passed the Babe.

"Move Over, Babe, Here Comes Henry." Remember?

I was there that night, and forty-six years later, it remains one of the most memorable experiences of my sporting life and career.

The anticipation had been building for two years. When the 1973 season began, it was obvious that Hank Aaron had a chance to break Babe Ruth's career homerun record that year, but he didn't.

He finished the season with 713 homeruns, one short of tying the great Bambino, two short of holding the long thought-to-be unbreakable record on his own.

But here we were in April 1974, on the cusp and edge of history, and everyone wanted to be there to see it happen. Like many others, I bought tickets to every game of the Braves' first home stand, intent on being there for the historic moment.

But there was one problem. Atlanta opened the season in Cincinnati.

The Braves planned on holding Aaron out of the Cincinnati

games to ensure that he would hit 714 and 715 in front of his home fans in Atlanta, but Major League Baseball, now simply called MLB, intervened and said Aaron had to play in Cincinnati to protect the integrity of the game.

It was a three-game series, as I recall, and the Braves did play him—for one game. But in that one game, he hit 714. Henry and the Babe were now tied. But there was still that all-important 715 for the record, and that would come in Atlanta, and I would be there.

It was a cool night. I can describe the atmosphere best by comparing it to the moments before the start of a college football playoff national championship game. It easily surpassed the World Series and the Super Bowl.

Aaron, of course, hit the homerun that night. Al Downing of the Dodgers threw it; Tom House caught it in the Braves' bullpen.

We cheered and cheered. Cheered and cheered. Big, long, loud, lusty cheers. It was that kind of night.

Two memories stand out about that night in addition to the moment the ball crossed the fence and the crowd reaction.

Milo Hamilton was the Braves' radio play-by-play announcer and insisted on calling the historic shot whenever it came. The Braves approved his request, which was more a demand than a request.

Whenever Aaron came to bat for what could be 714 or 715, Hamilton was to take over play-by-play duties from Ernie

Johnson, his announcing partner, for that one at-bat, and then Johnson would resume calling the game.

As it worked out, Aaron hit 715 early in the game, and Hamilton was on the call anyway. Hamilton's insistence on making the call always seemed a bit selfish to me. I loved his call then, and I love it now, but knowing Hamilton's attitude taints it a bit. Just a bit but tainted still.

The second thing I remember is how much I wanted to talk to my daddy, how much I wanted to share the moment with him, to tell him what it was like to have been there for 715. Not long after Aaron hit it, I left to find a pay phone.

I wasn't the only one who wanted to share the moment. There were long lines at every pay phone in the stadium. Cell phones were unheard of at this time; they were far, far into the future.

I finally got Daddy. I don't remember what I said or what he said, and it isn't important. We connected. We got to share the moment. That's what mattered then, and it matters still.

Hank Aaron went on to hit 755 homeruns, none bigger than he hit forty-six years ago tonight, April 8, 1974.

And in my view, he's still the all-time Homerun King.

The Ultimate Question

Only three words long, it is the most important question ever asked.

It is the question that has been asked and pondered since man first put foot upon the earth. It is the question the serpent asked Eve and the question Eve asked the serpent. It is the question Adam asked, or should have asked, Eve. And it is our question often, if not every day.

It is the question Pilate asked Jesus: "What is truth?"

What is truth? Interesting isn't it that Jesus never responded to Pilate. He left Pilate to decide—as he leaves us to decide.

Pilate walked out and offered the crowd a choice: "Barabbas or Jesus?" We are offered that same choice today, the way of Jesus or the way of the world.

Which do we choose?

As Mary put the message from the angel into her heart

and pondered it, so let us put Pilate's question in our heart and ponder it. "What is truth?"

How we answer that question will determine how we spend our lives.

What is truth?

The Four E's

Easter was the favorite time of the year for the Four E's. Time to sell Easter lilies to any and everybody they knew and to anybody they happened to run into at McDaniel's, the Yellow Front store, or the Piggly Wiggly.

They called people who lived out of town but had some connection, no matter how small or how remote, to the church. Their goal every year was to sell more Easter lilies than the year before, and they usually did. Persistence paid off.

I don't remember what they sold for—five dollars I'd guess. That came with the understanding that buyers could pick up their lily from the church sanctuary after the eleven o'clock services on Easter Sunday.

Or, if the buyer lived out of town, their lily would be carried to the cemetery and placed on the grave of the loved one they wanted to remember. Kind of like a big Decoration Day. You country folks will know what I mean by that.

My brother and I carried lots and lots of lilies to that little town cemetery over the years, more than I could count then or care to remember now, tromping through the graveyard, looking for the resting place of people we didn't even know. And you never stepped on a grave, always around or over it.

"Oh, that's Mr. So-and-So's great-aunt," we were told, and off we'd go, not knowing who Mr. So-and-So was, much less where Mr. So-and-So and his great-aunt might be buried.

Our only guides were names on the headstones of family plots. Unfortunately, there were lots and lots of people with the same last name buried in that cemetery, Sullivans, Browns, Prices, Burkhalters, Elmores. Oh, those Elmores! They were buried everywhere. Or so it seemed.

Finding the different graves was time-consuming, maddening, and frustrating, but we got it done because the Four E's said we would get it done.

The Four E's, as they were known, were Estelle, Eunice, Ethel, and Elizabeth. Estelle and Elizabeth were elementary school teachers, Eunice, a nurse, Ethel, a homemaker, or, as we would say today, a stay-at-home mom. They went to the same church and had children about the same age in the same school and, more often than not, in the same Sunday school class at church.

They did everything together. They were the movers and shakers among the women of that little town. If you wanted something done or needed to get something done, contact one of the Four E's. They would get it done.

They burned up that party line. Those were the days when telephones had party lines, shared lines rather than individual lines. More than one person or household on a single line. Remember? Did you ever listen in?

No matter what it was, if it was good for the church, the school, or the town, they would get it done—or their husbands and children, under their direction, would get it done.

The Four E's were a close-knit group. They talked together, played together as it were, and shared their lives together. The little town in which they lived was better for it.

A church event, a school event, someone who had lost everything in a fire or experienced a death in the family, the Four E's were there. Just as sure as day follows night, the Four E's were there. It mattered not what church the family attended or what part of town they lived in, the Four E's were always there.

They were a happy band. They laughed a lot, smiled a lot, and teased a lot. They must have had their differences, all people do, but no one would ever have known it. They were always together, usually doing good. They were an unselfish bunch.

They were special ladies, the Four E's—Estelle, Eunice, Ethel, and Elizabeth. Their little town and the people in it were better because they were there, because they cared, and because they were willing, if not eager, to show it.

They wanted people in the town to know they were loved and cared about, especially the shut-ins. They had good hearts, the Four E's. Good hearts.

Every time I see an Easter lily this week, I will think about the Four E's and all those dad-gum Easter lilies my brother and I had to carry to that cemetery so many years ago. But I do miss them—not the lilies, the 4 E's.

And I'd gladly carry lily after lily to the cemetery this year if it meant I could see them, especially one of them, one more time, and tell them how blessed I am to have had them in my life.

We all were, all of us in that small town we called home.

Young Tanner Bailey

All this talk about young Tanner Bailey, quarterback of the Gordo Green Wave—and it is "Green Wave" not "Greenwave"—getting scholarship offers from both Auburn and Alabama brings to mind an old story about his great-grandparents, Mr. James Bailey and Miss Edna Earl.

Tanner never knew them, and that's unfortunate. They were good people. Mr. James ran a little grocery store in downtown, such as it was, Gordo. Miss Edna Earl worked at home. She was a homemaker, a housewife as they were called in those days.

They were our across-the-street neighbors. They were good neighbors. Mr. James always welcomed a little boy looking for something to do into his store for a sit-down visit.

Miss Edna Earl was always ready to make that same little boy feel welcome in their home. She would always support school projects, and when summer came and that little boy went around the neighborhood collecting coat hangers to sell to Mr. Corbett Mills's cleaners for a penny a piece, she was always his biggest donor.

All of this happened a long time ago before air-conditioning and streetlights that illuminated the skies as well as the heretofore darkened streets.

These were the days when folks sat in the front yard in aluminum folding chairs and visited at night. Mr. James and Miss Edna Earl would sit on their porch, the Housels in our front yard, and Mr. Marvin Price and Miss Kacy, who lived next door to the Baileys, would sit in their screened-in porch.

We could always tell when Mr. Marvin was there by the orange glow of his ever-present cigar.

They talked about everything, slowly, quietly, sometime with long pauses, never confrontational. They talked about what was going on in the town, people in the town, but never in a negative way—church, baseball, politics, football, and whatever else. Good front yard visiting. Visiting as it used to be and ought to be again.

My brother and I, too young to enter the conversation, just listened and looked for shooting stars and the Echo satellite.

Satellites were big deals in those days, and when we spotted one moving slowly across the sky, everybody came out to see it. Even Miss Kacy, who rarely left the porch for anything.

Those were the days.

Then came television.

Mr. James and Miss Edna Earl had one of the first television sets in the town and absolutely the first TV in our little part of the world.

My mother, ever the curious one, had never seen a television before. Every night or so, with me in tow, she would slip quietly across the street and stand in the Bailey's front yard, looking through the window at the wonderful invention called television, even though it was little more than moving shadows on a small, fuzzy, white, snowy screen.

But it was television. It was the future, and she wanted to see it, to be a part of the wonderful amazing world to come. Little did we know. Little could we have imagined.

Daddy would never go. He was afraid we would get caught and he would be embarrassed. We never got caught. And this, to my knowledge, this is the first time in more than sixty years this story has been told.

They're all gone now—Momma, Daddy, Mr. James, Miss Edna Earle, Mr. Marvin, Miss Kacy.

Their sons, David, Raymond, and Ken, Ken Bailey, Tanner's grandfather, are all retired. And now along comes young Tanner, being recruited by Auburn, Alabama, and many others.

Naturally, I would like for him to come to Auburn, but we, all of us, should want what's best for him, be it at Auburn, Alabama, or another place of his choosing.

Wherever he goes, whenever I hear his name, I will think back to those long-ago summer nights, standing secretly and silently in his great-grandparents' front yard, watching television for the first time.

Mr. James and Miss Edna Earl would be proud of Tanner. So proud.

I've never met the young man, and I'm proud of him. All because of watching television from his great-grandparents' front yard so long ago. It is a tie that binds.

I Hear the Train a Coming

It happens early every morning about three o'clock. That's when I get up to go to what some people call "the smallest room in the house."

While standing in that small room, off in the distance I hear the sound of a train whistle. Not the long, low, mournful sound country singers sing about but one of those "I'm coming through" whistles—clear, strong, and direct.

I've often thought about where the train is, at the Dean Road crossing, the East University Drive crossing, or maybe the Tiger Town crossing. But it matters not. The years fall away by decades, and I am a ten-year-old boy again, my dream, my only dream, to be a railroad engineer.

To blow that whistle would be the grandest, most glorious thing in all the world. No higher calling than to blow that whistle and feel the power of that engine surge under my control. Life couldn't get any better than that.

I, like most boys my age, had a fascination with trains.

Electric trains, especially Lionel trains, were great to play with, but they couldn't come close to the real thing, the magnificence and power of those red and yellow GM&O engines that rolled through our little town twice a day.

We lived about a block and a half from the railroad tracks that ran through a cut next to Mr. George Price's house.

When I heard that first wail of the train whistle, I would run as fast as my chubby little legs would carry me to the top of the cut to see the train go by. It was a magical and mystical time.

When we pretty much learned the train schedule, my town buddies, usually Frank Elmore and Larry Blakeney, and I would go to the cut and wait for the train to go by. We would wave at the engineer, and if we were lucky, he would wave back to us. Sometimes he might even blow the whistle for us. Those were the really good days.

We were bold and adventurous boys, but we had our limits. There were some things we just wouldn't do. One of them was putting silver dollars on the tracks. Silver dollars, parallel to each other, one on each rail, would stop the train on the spot. Or so we had been told. It was a moot point because we didn't have many silver dollars in those days.

But pennies, nickels, dimes, and quarters, those were another matter. We often put those coins on the track, always the same kind of coin, to see what would happen, to see if they would slow the train down even a little bit.

They never did, but as soon as the caboose—these were the days when trains had cabooses—rumbled by, we ran or slid down the steep hill of that cut to find those coins. They were treasured items. I wish I had one of them now, even at seventy-one years of age. Strange what we treasure as we age.

The best of times came when the train switched cars on and off the side tracks in our little town.

The train would stop right were we stood, at eye level, only a few yards away from the engine and the engineer. On good days, on great days, the engineer would talk to us, and we felt like we were on the doorsteps of heaven. And when he blew that whistle, sometimes just for us, it was like the trumpets of angels.

It couldn't get any better than that. But it did.

I have lived a good life, a very good life, far better than any I could have imagined at that time. Far better.

But every night, in the wee, small hours of morning, I hear that faraway train whistle, and I'm a kid again.

And part of me wonders, just wonders, what it would have been like if my childhood dream had come true.

GM&O engine of the 1950s

Would You Do It Over Again?

Do you ever think, just for an instant, for a moment, how nice and meaningful it would be to go back and spend a day, even an afternoon, with your parents as in days of old?

To wake up in the morning, have a bowl of cereal, Kellogg's Frosted Flakes or Sugar Corn Pops, watch a little TV, the *Today* show with Dave Garroway and J. Fred Muggs, then walk downtown to the store, in my case a hardware store.

Hanging around, out of the way and out of sight, listening to the old men talk. And thinking, *I don't ever want to be that old* ...

But now I am that old. And older.

To walk to the post office, get the mail, then ride home for lunch, "dinner" as we called it, with Daddy in that old black Ford Fairlane.

To ride past the chinaberry tree where I used to sit on the sidewalk and wait for him to come home when I was too young to walk to town alone.

To sit at the little round table in the den with Momma, Daddy, and my little brother, Raymond, eating some of Hattie Blair's (Hat-T's) good cooking. Nothing better then; nothing better now.

Watch a little more TV, perhaps *Search for Tomorrow* or *The Guiding Light,* the nuances of which I had no way of understanding.

Watch Benny Carle and the *Circle Six Ranch* at four and then walk back downtown to spend the rest of the afternoon at the store with Daddy, the old men now gone. Maybe going across the street to see Mr. Marvin or down the street to see Mr. Harold, hearing about Auburn.

Coming home around six o'clock or later, eating leftovers for supper, taking out the garbage and feeding the dogs, Bullet, Lassie, and later Spot. The names weren't very original, but that didn't matter; we loved them anyway. And they loved us.

Then a little more TV, a Western at 6:30, followed by a variety show, perhaps Perry Como or Andy Williams at seven or eight.

On a good night, there would be comedy, Red Skelton, Jackie Gleason, *I Love Lucy, December Bride,* or a quiz show, *To Tell the Truth* or *What's My Line?. The $64,000 Question* with Hal March and Teddy Nadler was still in the future, as were Eliot Ness and *The Untouchables.*

Watching TV and talking with Momma and Daddy, about everything and nothing, about nothing and everything.

The joy and satisfaction of staying up late, watching TV alone. That meant I was growing up.

To go to bed in that world and wake up living once again the lives we live today.

Do you ever think about things like that?

The blessing in all of this, of course, is that we had the kind of childhood that makes us want to go back and relive some of those times again, just for a little while, a day, an afternoon.

Thank you, Daddy. Thank you, Momma.

I miss you.

All I Know, All I've Ever Learned

Commencement Speech given at Auburn University's Graduation, May 7, 2017

Mr. President, Members of the Board of Trustees, Distinguished Faculty, Guests, and Above All to You Who Are About to Become Graduates of Auburn University:

I am very mindful of what Abraham Lincoln said in his Gettysburg Address:

"The world will little note nor long remember what we say here, but the world can never forget what they did here …"

I am in much the same situation. The world will little note nor long remember what I say here, but the world can never forget what you did here.

I cannot remember one single word spoken at my graduation, but I will always remember the day I graduated.

I am also fully aware of what was described as one of Winston Churchill's most effective addresses. Speaking to students at his alma mater, Harrow School, in 1941 during World War II, Churchill is supposed to have said, "Never give up. Never, never, never give up" and sat down.

The historians among us tell us his actual words were slightly different. For today's purposes, we will go with the myth, the legend, Churchill saying "never, never, never, never give up ..." In keeping with that theme and number, I want to encourage you to "Never Give Up" on *Four things*.

What you are about to hear is the culmination of all my learning and more than 50 years at Auburn:

Never Give Up on Yourself

You are capable of doing good—even great and lasting things. You are capable of making everything you touch better. Do it.

Never underestimate your ability.

48 years ago, a young man named Jay Gouge from Waycross, GA sat where you are sitting in a building not too far from here waiting to receive his degree in Horticulture.

Never, in his wildest dreams and imaginations did he think he would be sitting here as President of Auburn University, his alma mater and soon to be your alma mater.

And, Dr. Gouge, today, as you preside over your last graduation, I, and all Auburn people, thank you for your leadership and your contribution to our alma mater, the school we love and care about.

You have made us better.

We thank you, and we wish you well. As they used to say in that long ago time back in Waycross, "You done good boy … you made us proud."

(To the Graduates) Now, you may not become President of Auburn University, but you can make a difference wherever life's journey takes you.

General George Washington, the Father of Our Country, said, "Perseverance and spirit have done wonders in all ages …"

It gave birth to a nation, and it can carry you to places beyond your wildest dreams and your ability to imagine.

Never Give Up on Your Fellowman and the Power of Forgiveness.

We've all heard it said, "Forgive and Forget," and we have all been told or understood that it comes from the Bible.

Not so.

It comes from Shakespeare. *King Lear* Act 4, Scene 7, Line 85.

We aren't made to forget, but we are made to forgive.

In forgiving, we no longer allow the hurts, slights, grudges and anger of the past, the scars and bruises of the past, to cripple our relationship with others.

And we no longer allow the past to rob us of the joys and happiness the future is sure to hold.

Frank, a character in M.L. Stedman's wonderful book *Light Between the Oceans,* put it this way:

"I choose to forgive. I can let myself rot in the past, spend my time hating people, or I can forgive.

You only have to forgive once. To resent, you have to do it all day, every day. You have to keep remembering all the bad things.

"I would have to make a list," he said, "a very long list and make sure I hated the people on that list the right amount and that I did a good enough job of hating.

"We always have a choice, all of us."

Never give up on your fellowman. We are not perfect and you are not perfect, but together you can accomplish great things.

Accomplish those great things.

Never Give Up on Learning

As Shakespeare's Hamlet said to Horatio, "There are more things in heaven and earth than art dreamt of in your philosophy," and I might add your learning.

The degree you are about to receive doesn't mean you have all the answers. It means that you have successfully completed a course of study designed to help you know where and how to start looking for the answers. This is but a beginning.

Seek those things of which Hamlet spoke.

Seek the truth.

And choose to believe that truth, no matter how you feel and no matter what you want to believe. Believe the truth.

Don't be afraid of where the truth may lead, in faith or in fact.

Make that journey with Hamlet and Horatio, and with the scientists, philosophers, theologians and educators of this day and in the days to come.

Seek the truth, and do not be afraid of where it may lead.

Never Give Up on Auburn

Whatever you do, wherever you go, you will always be part of Auburn, and Auburn will always be part of you.

Auburn didn't just spring into being when you enrolled and walked these hallowed halls. For more than 150 years Auburn men and women had been trying to make Auburn better, to make Auburn as good as it could be, awaiting your arrival.

Now it's your turn.

It is now your responsibility to make Auburn better for those who follow you, for the next generation, for your sons and daughters who will tread where you have trod.

Auburn has helped make you who you are.

Believe in Auburn. Love it and make it better for those who follow you. Make it better for your sons and daughters and their sons and daughters.

Make Auburn better.

In Closing

In closing let me say to you what Dick Smith, director of the Kennedy Space Center and Auburn alum, said to Hank Hartsfield and Ken Mattingly, two Auburn astronauts, as they lifted off on the final test flight of the Space Shuttle Columbia:

"God Speed and War Eagle!"

Each life has a beginning, middle and an end. What's important is not how long but how deeply and fully we live …

Drink of the cup deeply, my friends, for it passes your way but once.

Epilogue

Contentment.

Sure is nice to be at home, sitting in my chair, cat in my lap, watching football, listening to the rain, watching the leaves fall.

Free at last, free at last.

Life is good.

I am blessed.

-30-